# BACH PERSPECTIVES

VOLUME 3
Creative Responses to Bach
from Mozart to Hindemith

# BACH PERSPECTIVES

VOLUME THREE

## Editorial Board

Published by the
University of Nebraska Press
in association with the
American Bach Society

# Bach

# *Perspectives*

VOLUME THREE

Creative Responses to Bach
from Mozart to Hindemith

*Edited by Michael Marissen*

University of Nebraska Press, Lincoln and London 1998

# CONTENTS

# PREFACE

Although there is a fairly extensive secondary literature on what composers have said or written about Bach's music, less attention has been devoted to the forms that their responses have taken in works of music. The present volume is designed to help fill that gap. These essays focus for the most part on compositional reception, but the title's "creative responses" is to be understood to include music-theoretical and biographical materials as well.

With the exception of William Kinderman's article, the contents of this volume stem from the April 1996 meeting of the American Bach Society at the University of California at Berkeley. By the generosity of the executive and advisory boards of the American Bach Society, and in particular of its president at the time, Don O. Franklin, I was granted considerable leeway in organizing the lectures for the conference. Hoping to make those lectures, and thereby this volume, appealing not only to Bach specialists but also to non-specialists, I worked to secure leading scholars with special expertise on figures responding to Bach after his death in 1750. The contributions by Ludwig Finscher, Walter Frisch, Stephen Hinton, and Robert Marshall were delivered in a session of invited papers; the essay by Thomas Christensen stems from a free session.

In an introductory article, Ludwig Finscher offers a broad, succinct survey of much of the terrain. Thomas Christensen shows that Bach's first disciples each claimed authority from their master for their opposing assessments of music in general, and that it is in fact difficult to pin down Bach's place among the music theorists. In an area as rich as Bach's music, there seems to have been something for every theorist. Robert Marshall argues that Mozart's deep involvement with Bach's music probably stems from a much earlier period than the usually cited interaction of the 1780s in Vienna and Leipzig. William Kinderman shows that Beethoven, too, probably came to know and assimilate Bach's music earlier than is generally thought, and that all aspects of Beethoven's mature style are heavily indebted to Bach. Walter Frisch compares an older sort of historicism in Brahms's Bach reception with the development of musical modernism in succeeding generations. And, finally, Stephen Hinton traces Hindemith's apparently changing yet essentially consistent images of Bach.

I would like to thank Stephen Crist, Daniel Melamed, and Joshua Rifkin for advice and encouragement in the early stages of this project. In addition, I am extremely grateful to the American Bach Society and its presidents, Don O. Franklin and, now, George B. Stauffer, for their support.

*Michael Marissen*
Swarthmore, Pennsylvania

# ABBREVIATIONS

BDOK    Werner Neumann and Hans-Joachim Schulze, eds. 4 vols. *Bach-Dokumente*. Kassel: Bärenreiter; Leipzig: VEB Deutsche Verlag für Musik, 1963–78.

BR      Hans T. David and Arthur Mendel, eds. *The Bach Reader: A Life of Johann Sebastian Bach in Letters and Documents*. Rev. ed. New York: W. W. Norton, 1966.

BWV     Wolfgang Schmieder, ed. *Thematisch-systematisches Verzeichnis der musikalischen Werke von Johann Sebastian Bach (Bach-Werke-Verzeichnis)*. Rev. ed. Wiesbaden: Breitkopf & Härtel, 1990.

HWV     [Händel-Werke-Verzeichnis.] Bernd Baselt. *Thematisch-systematisches Verzeichnis: Instrumentalmusik, Pasticci und Fragmente*. Händel-Handbuch, vol. 3. Kassel: Bärenreiter, 1986.

P       Partitur. [Music score, abbreviation used by the SBB.]

SBB     Staatsbibliothek zu Berlin—Stiftung Preussischer Kulturberitz.

WOO     Werk ohne Opuszahl. [Work without opus number.]

# BACH PERSPECTIVES

VOLUME 3

Creative Responses to Bach
from Mozart to Hindemith

# Bach's Posthumous Role in Music History

### Ludwig Finscher

O n 21 March 1985 a Berlin radio station celebrated Bach's three hundredth birthday with an all-night program featuring Bach's music. The highlight of this program was an open-air performance, around midnight, of "Jesu meine Freude." The choir stood on a rostrum, at the foot of the Kaiser-Wilhelm-Gedächtniskirche ruins, surrounded by the still-raging traffic. It was an unforgettable moment when they sang the lines "tobe, Welt, und springe; ich steh hier und singe in gar sich'rer Ruh" against the traffic noise, the truly raging world. For one moment, the work of art had found a new place in everyday life, and text and music were transformed from a masterpiece in the Imaginary Museum of Musical Works into something quite different: a strong and vital voice of cultural identity in a hostile world.[1] The extraordinary effect of this event, of course, was largely due to the jarring clash between the external circumstances and the sheer quality of the work of art. But there were also some other factors. The effect would not have been the same with a hypothetical motet by Telemann on the same text, even if the musical difference between the two motets would not have been as substantial as we customarily take for granted when comparing Bach with any other composer of his time. No German radio station would have cared to stage an all-night tricentennial Telemann program on 14 March 1981: Bach is generally considered a rather special composer, if not the greatest composer of all time.

This attitude is rooted not only in fact but in fiction, not only in the special quality of Bach's music but also in a history of reception that in Germany from its beginnings combined genuine admiration of the composer with political

1. Andre Malraux, *Le musée imaginaire de la sculpture mondiale*, 3 vols. (Paris: Gallimard, 1952–54); Lydia Goehr, *The Imaginary Museum of Musical Works: An Essay in the Philosophy of Music* (Oxford: Clarendon Press, 1992).

1

aspirations: to set him above all foreign composers, to make him a symbol of German Art (whatever that was taken to be at a given historical moment), and to turn him into an icon of cultural identity for a nation that—around the time of Bach's death—for the first time began consciously to suffer from its lack of political unity and power.

The facts are well known. Already in 1737, Lorenz Mizler held Bach to be a keyboard virtuoso who, together with Handel, had lifted German musician-ship to the highest rank, exceeding all French and Italian keyboard players.[2] Even Johann Adolph Scheibe saw in Bach a master (again primarily a keyboard master) "by whom we can certainly defy all foreigners," extolling the Italian Concerto as a masterpiece that foreign composers would strive only in vain to imitate.[3] In 1751 Friedrich Wilhelm Marpurg wrote that, just as Greece had but one Homer and Rome but one Virgil, so Germany had but one Bach; in 1778 Johann Nikolaus Forkel called Corelli, Scarlatti, Caldara, and Rameau mere schoolboys when compared with his hero.[4]

2. *M. Lorenz Mizlers Musikalische Bibliothek*, Dritter Theil (Leipzig, 1737), 9–10, quoted in BDOK 2, no. 404: "Wo können andere Nationen solche Clavieristen aufweisen, als Händel und unser Herr Bach allhier. . . . So weit man also in der Musik nur immer gekommen ist, so weit sind auch die Deutschen gekommen, und haben sich vor anderen Nationen den Vorzug erwor-ben." See also my "Händel und Bach: Zur Geschichte eines musikhistoriographischen Topos," in *Göttinger Händel-Beiträge* III, ed. Hans Joachim Marx (Kassel: Bärenreiter, 1989), 9–25.

3. *Johann Adolph Scheibens . . . Critischer Musicus: Neue, vermehrte und verbesserte Auflage* (Leip-zig, 1745), 637–38, quoted in BDOK 2, no. 463: "Ein so großer Meister der Musik, als Herr Bach ist, der sich insonderheit des Claviers fast ganz allein bemächtiget hat, und mit dem wir den Ausländern ganz sicher trotzen können, mußte es auch seyn, uns in dieser Setzart ein solches Stück [BWV 971] zu liefern, welches den Nacheifer aller unserer großen Componisten verdienet, von den Ausländern aber nur vergebens wird nachgeahmet werden."

4. Anonymous [Friedrich Wilhelm Marpurg], *Gedanken über die welschen Tonkünstler . . .* (Hal-berstadt, 1751), 20–21, quoted in BDOK 3, no. 642: "wie Griechenland nur einen Homer, und Rom nur einen Virgil gehabt: So wird Deutschland wohl nur einen Bach gehabt haben, dem in der vorigen Zeit . . . in ganz Europa keiner gleich gekommen ist, und den in der Folgewelt keiner übertreffen wird," and earlier in the same text: "Uns gilt das kleinste Werk, darinn man Bachen schmeckt, / Mehr, als was Welschlands Kiel noch jemahls ausgeheckt" (ironically, writ-ten not in a "German" meter but in alexandrines—lines of iambic hexameter used in French heroic verse). Johann Nicolaus Forkel, *Musikalisch-kritische Bibliothek*, vol. 2 (Gotha, 1778), 157, quoted in BDOK 3, no. 834: "Gegen diesen großen Mann sind Corelli, [Domenico] Scarlatti, Caldara und Rameau, so groß auch ihre Verdienste an sich betrachtet seyn mögen, noch wahre Schulknaben."

The first peak in this development was, of course, Forkel's biography of 1802, dedicated "to all patriotic admirers of true musical art."[5] By now Bach had become the greatest composer of all times and places, the glory of the German nation, someone whose towering genius would take centuries to understand fully. Still, very little of Bach's oeuvre was known, and less yet outside of the limited circles of connoisseurs and professional musicians. But the highly ideological Bach Image became further developed in a burgeoning theoretical discourse, something that, after the turn of the century, was even more widely disseminated, and popularized, by music journalism. General tendencies helped: the Romantic discovery of History (and Bach had by now become an old master), the Romantic ideology of instrumental music as formulated by E. T. A. Hoffmann (himself a Bach admirer, who allowed his Kapellmeister Kreisler to experience Bach's keyboard music practically as a drug), and the renewal of Protestant Pietism.[6] Goethe's famous statement on Bach must be seen in this highly complicated context—and, when seen in this context, it loses something of its purported originality and profundity.[7]

5. Johann Nikolaus Forkel, *Ueber Johann Sebastian Bachs Leben, Kunst und Kunstwerke: Für patriotische Verehrer echter musikalischer Kunst* (Leipzig, 1802).

6. Ernst Theodor Amadeus Hoffmann, *Johannes Kreisler's, des Kapellmeisters, musikalische Leiden*, written in 1809 or 1810, and first published in *Allgemeine musikalische Zeitung Leipzig* 12, no. 52, 26 September 1810; later printed in *Fantasiestücke in Callot's Manier: Erster Teil* (Bamberg, 1814). Hoffmann writes with regard to the "Goldberg" Variations: "Die Quartblätter dehnten sich plötzlich aus zu einem Riesenfolio, wo tausend Imitationen und Ausführungen jenes Themas geschrieben standen, die ich abspielen mußte. Die Noten wurden lebendig und flimmerten und hüpften um mich her—elektrisches Feuer fuhr durch die Fingerspitzen in die Tasten—der Geist, von dem es ausströmte, überflügelte die Gedanken—der ganze Saal hing voll dichten Dufts, in dem die Kerzen düstrer und düstrer brannten—zuweilen sah eine Nase heraus, zuweilen ein paar Augen: aber sie verschwanden gleich wieder." Walter Blankenburg, "Die Berliner Wiederaufführung der Matthäus-Passion: Denkmal oder Programm?" in *Bachtage Berlin: Vorträge 1970 bis 1981*, ed. Günther Wagner (Neuhausen-Stuttgart: Hänssler, 1985), 23–31.

7. Draft of a letter to Carl Friedrich Zelter, 21 June 1827, in *Werke*, Weimar Edition, IV/42, 376: "Ich sprach mir's aus: als wenn die ewige Harmonie sich mit sich selbst unterhielte, wie sich's etwa in Gottes Busen, kurz vor der Weltschöpfung, möchte zugetragen haben. So bewegte sich's auch in meinem Innern und es war mir als wenn ich weder Ohren, am wenigsten Augen, und weiter keine übrigen Sinne besäße noch brauchte." Cf. Friedrich Smend, *Goethes Verhältnis zu Bach* (Berlin-Darmstadt: Merseburger, 1955); reprinted in Smend, *Bach-*

Time and again, political overtones can be heard. The famous 1829 revival of the St. Matthew Passion in Berlin was hailed by Adolf Bernhard Marx as the discovery of the "greatest and best work of the greatest tone poet," and even as the "greatest and holiest work of musical art," an act that would inaugurate a new epoch of mankind.[8] The performance—in the concert hall of the Singakademie (i.e., in secular surroundings)—was likened to a religious ceremony, and Fanny Mendelssohn reports that people felt as if they were taking part in a church service, the audience having responded in profoundest silence and most solemn piety. At the same time, however, the performance formed part of Marx's battle for German music and against the Prussian Generalmusikdirektor Spontini—a war that was, beyond its artistic purposes, a surrogate for the political and even military war that was impossible to wage under the conditions of the Restoration era.

To put it bluntly: the early history of Bach reception, up to the point in the early nineteenth century when the composers took over, is in large part the history of the shaping of an ideology, albeit an ideology buttressed by the incomparable quality of Bach's music. Likewise, it is the history of an almost exclusively theoretical reception, a discourse that has the advantage of being

---

*Studien: Gesammelte Reden und Aufsätze*, ed. Christoph Wolff (Kassel: Bärenreiter, 1969), 212-36; Walter Wiora, *Goethes Wort über Bach*, in *Hans Albrecht in memoriam*, ed. Wilfried Brennecke and Hans Haase (Kassel: Bärenreiter, 1962), 179-91; reprinted in Hellmut Kühn and Christoph-Hellmut Mahling, eds., *Historische und systematische Musikwissenschaft: Ausgewählte Aufsätze von Walter Wiora* (Tutzing: Hans Schneider, 1972), 251-67; Hans-Georg Gadamer, *Bach und Weimar* (Weimar: Herm. Böhlhaus Nachf., 1946); reprinted in Gadamer, *Gesammelte Werke*, vol. 9 (Tübingen: J. C. B. Mohr [Paul Siebeck], 1993), 142-49; and Dieter Borchmeyer, "'Götterwort der Töne': Goethes Theorie der Musik," *Freiburger Universitätsblätter* 133 (1996): 109-34, esp. 129-31.

8. *Berliner Allgemeine musikalische Zeitung*, 28 February 1829: "des größten und besten Werks des größten Tondichters," "des größten und heiligsten Gebildes der Tonkunst," "Wie die erste Morgensonne nach den Nebellasten der Sündfluth verkündet sie einen neuen leuchtenden Tag." For these and the following details, see Martin Geck, *Die Wiederentdeckung der Matthäuspassion im 19. Jahrhundert: Die zeitgenössischen Dokumente und ihre ideengeschichtliche Deutung* (Regensburg: Gustav Bosse, 1967), 9; Gottfried Eberle, "'Du hast mir Arbeit gemacht': Schwierigkeiten der Bach-Rezeption im Umkreis der Sing-Akademie zu Berlin," *Jahrbuch des Staatlichen Instituts für Musikforschung Preußischer Kulturbesitz 1993*, 88-105; Arno Forchert, "'Die Hauptstadt von Sebastian Bach': Berliner Bach-Traditionen zwischen Klassik und Romantik," *Jahrbuch des Staatlichen Instituts für Musikforschung Preußischer Kulturbesitz 1995*, 9-28.

delivered in print (affecting the way historical evidence is presented) but the disadvantage of being separated from the contemporary history of musical composition. It is not by happenstance that most studies of the history of Bach reception center on this verbal evidence, and that one of the earliest and most comprehensive of these, Friedrich Blume's *Two Centuries of Bach*, has very little—and nothing illuminating—to say on the way Bach was received by later composers.[9] This state of affairs has to be kept in mind. When we now turn to the composers' reception of Bach, we turn to a virtually unwritten history.[10]

The composers' response to Bach and his oeuvre runs along its own lines, mostly independent of the theorists' reception. Nevertheless, there is a theorists' branch among the composers themselves, consisting of what the composers said (or allegedly said) about Bach and what Bach meant to them. There is little reason to think that composers talk differently from other people and that they are blessedly untainted by ideology, and so it comes as no surprise to find a number of statements from them that approach Bach ideology. To quote a few examples: Richard Wagner said that Bach is "the history of the German spirit's innermost life during the abominable century of the German nation's total eclipse." [11] The political overtones can be heard distinctly, and there is once again the time-honored counterpoint of the dichotomy between the greatness of the German spirit and the misery of German reality. Brahms said that the loss of all other music would grieve him but that the loss of Bach's music would make him inconsolable.[12] He also said that the three greatest ex-

9. Friedrich Blume, *J. S. Bach im Wandel der Geschichte* (Kassel: Bärenreiter, 1947), reprinted in Blume, *Syntagma Musicologicum: Gesammelte Reden und Schriften*, ed. Martin Ruhnke (Kassel: Bärenreiter, 1963), 412–47 and 897–98; trans. by Stanley Godman as *Two Centuries of Bach* (London: Oxford University Press, 1950).

10. There are some essays dealing with single chapters of this history; e.g., Frank Schneider, "Bach als Quelle im Strom der Moderne," *Jahrbuch des Staatlichen Instituts für Musikforschung Preußischer Kulturbesitz 1994*, 110–25; Christian Martin Schmidt, "Die Musikgeschichte des 19. Jahrhunderts kann man ohne Bach nicht schreiben," ibid., 96–125.

11. "Was ist deutsch? (1878)," in *Gesammelte Schriften und Dichtungen*, vol. 10 (Leipzig, 1883), 36–53, at p. 47: "Er ist die Geschichte des innerlichsten Lebens des deutschen Geistes während des grauenvollen Jahrhunderts der gänzlichen Erloschenheit des deutschen Volkes."

12. Quotation from Blume, *Syntagma Musicologicum*, 437 n. 11. Blume gives no source; the dependability of his quotation is questionable, since some other quotations in the same paragraph are incorrect.

periences in his life had been his acquaintance with Schumann, the "year 70" (i.e., the French-German war and the subsequent foundation of the German Reich), and the production of the Bach-Ausgabe.[13]

Fortunately, there are various statements besides Beethoven's rather feeble pun "not *brook* [in German, *Bach*], but *ocean* should be his name."[14] What some of the younger composers had to say—and only a few can be quoted here—can be divided into two sharply different ways of thinking and speaking: one creating an altogether mythological, cosmological, superhuman Bach (in this respect following Beethoven's metaphor from nature), and the other speaking soberly in terms of musical craft. The protagonist of the first approach is—not surprisingly—Wagner, who not only spoke of the counterpoint in the *Meistersinger* prelude as "applied Bach" and of the assembly of the Meistersingers (act 1, scene 3) as a "continuation of Bach," but also associated Bach's music, especially the Well-Tempered Clavier, with a sphinx, with rotating planets, and with a world before the dawn of mankind.[15] In a telling comparison to his fully conscious stylization of his own creative process (especially in his report on the *Rheingold* prelude's conception), he even imagined Bach's creative pro-

13. "Brief an Oskar von Hase (1893?)," in Johannes Brahms, *Briefwechsel*, vol.14, ed. Wilhelm Altmann (Berlin: Deutsche Brahms-Gesellschaft, 1920; reprint, Tutzing: Hans Schneider, 1974): "Jeder Mensch erlebt doch so ein paar Dinge, von denen er sich sagt, daß es doch der Mühe wert ist, in der Zeit gelebt zu haben. Für mich kann ich etwa die drei sagen: Nun, daß ich jung Schumann noch kennen gelernt habe—dann, nun, daß ich das Jahr 70 habe erleben dürfen—und nun wie in den ganzen letzten Jahren Bach durch Ihre Ausgabe immer höher und höher aufgestiegen ist." Quoted incorrectly in Blume, *Syntagma Musicologicum*, 436. See also Siegmund Helms, "Johannes Brahms und Johann Sebastian Bach," *Bach-Jahrbuch* 57 (1971): 13–81.

14. Reported (from a visit in 1825) by Karl Gottlieb Freudenberg, "Erinnerungen aus dem Leben eines alten Organisten," 1870, p.37, quoted in *Ludwig van Beethoven: Berichte der Zeitgenossen, Briefe und persönliche Aufzeichnungen*, ed. Albert Leitzmann, *Erster-Band: Berichte der Zeitgenossen* (Leipzig: Insel, 1921), 284: "Nicht Bach, sondern Meer sollte er heißen."

15. As reported by Cosima in her diaries (15 December 1878): Cosima Wagner, *Die Tagebücher*, ed. Martin Gregor-Dellin and Dietrich Mack (Munich-Zurich: Piper, 1976), 2:260. Martin Geck, "Richard Wagner und die ältere Musik," in *Die Ausbreitung des Historismus über die Musik*, ed. Walter Wiora (Regensburg: Gustav Bosse, 1969), 123–46. See also Carl Dahlhaus, "Wagner und Bach," in *Programmhefte der Bayreuther Festspiele 1985*, vol.7, *Der fliegende Holländer*, 1–18; reprint, Dahlhaus, *Klassische und romantische Musikästhetik* (Laaber: Laaber, 1988), 440–58.

cess as subconscious.[16] In the wake of Wagner's mythological event, and in the shadow of his dream image of Bach, stands Max Reger; behind his attempts to describe the indescribable—the beginning and end of all music, omnipotent father Bach, godfather of music, father of harmony—looms the subconscious quest for a father figure.[17] At the other end of the spectrum stands Schoenberg's sober claim that he had learned his craft above all from Mozart and Bach. What he said he had learned from Bach was contrapuntal thinking (i.e., the art of inventing configurations that can accompany themselves), the art of developing everything from a single entity and developing configurations from each other, and independence from the beat.[18] Finally, standing entirely by itself, in Hindemith's memorable lecture of 1950, is the image of Bach as a moral force.[19]

There is yet another point where composers came into contact with Bach: teaching. The Well-Tempered Clavier had become a fairly common vehicle for teaching piano and counterpoint already in the eighteenth century, at least in North and Central Germany, and the tradition continued and expanded considerably in the nineteenth century.[20] In this process, the boundaries between using the Well-Tempered Clavier as a tool for teaching and for demonstrating "erudite" virtuosity were not always clearly defined, and again moral or metaphysical ideas might enter into the proceedings. Christian Gottlob Neefe en-

16. See the meticulous presentation and interpretation of the evidence in Warren Darcy, *Wagner's Das Rheingold* (Oxford: Clarendon Press, 1993), 62-64. Wagner, *Die Tagebücher*, 2: 229 (13 November 1878): "unbewußt im Traum ist vieles von Bach niedergeschrieben; die unendliche Melodie ist da prädestiniert." See also Christoph Wolff, "Brahms, Wagner, and the Problem of Historicism in Nineteenth-Century Music: An Essay," in *Brahms Studies: Analytical and Historical Perspectives*, ed. George S. Bozarth (Oxford: Clarendon Press, 1990), 10.

17. "Anfang und Ende aller Musik, Allvater Bach, Musikgottvater, Urvater der Harmonie." Quotations in Johannes Lorenzen, *Max Reger als Bearbeiter Bachs* (Wiesbaden: Breitkopf & Härtel, 1982), 55. The last quotation ("Urvater der Harmonie") was taken over verbatim from Beethoven's letter to Franz Anton Hoffmeister of 15 January 1801.

18. "Nationale Musik (1931)," in Schoenberg, *Stil und Gedanke: Aufsätze zur Musik*, ed. Ivan Vojtech (Frankfurt am Main: Suhrkamp, 1976), 250-54, at p.253.

19. "Johann Sebastian Bach: Ein verpflichtendes Erbe," lecture for the Hamburg Bach celebrations, 12 September 1950, in Hindemith, *Aufsätze—Vorträge—Reden*, ed. Giselher Schubert (Zurich-Mainz: Atlantis Musikbuch-Verlag, 1994), 253-70.

20. For a survey, see the relevant chapters in Martin Zenck, *Die Bach-Rezeption des späten Beethoven* (Stuttgart: Franz Steiner, 1986).

couraged his piano pupil, the thirteen-year-old Ludwig van Beethoven, to play large parts of the collection, and this was considered quite exceptional.[21] Similarly, the eight-year-old Brahms was brought to the pieces by his first piano teacher, Otto F. W. Cossel.[22] And the sixteen-year-old Clara Wieck played "every fugue by Bach, in any key one wished," much to the admiration of Carl Loewe.[23] When she married Robert Schumann, two Bach enthusiasts were matched up. With Schumann, the reception process was exalted to an ethical level; he believed that Bach's music would have a morally empowering effect.[24]

By the turn of the century, Bach had become ubiquitous. The historian and writer on music Karl Storck, in his proposed ideal private music library, named as a foundation for every music-loving piano player the works of Bach and especially the Well-Tempered Clavier—something toward which, however, one had gradually to work one's way.[25] (In my own family, a typical German middle-class household without exaggerated cultural ambitions, but with three piano-playing daughters, it was just like that.) And inevitably, we are reminded of Max Weber's essay on the sociology of music, with its penetrating interpretation of the history of equal temperament as part of the occidental

21. See the well-known report in Carl Friedrich Cramer, *Magazin der Musik, erster Jahrgang*, Hamburg 1783; reprinted and translated frequently; see BDOK 3, nos. 874–75. Neefe is generally considered to be the author of this report, but there is no proof for this. See also Zenck, *Die Bach-Rezeption*, 128.

22. Heinz Becker, *Brahms* (Stuttgart and Weimar: J. B. Metzler, 1993).

23. Letter from Loewe to his wife, 29 July 1835, published in *Dr. Carl Loewe's Selbstbiographie, bearbeitet von Carl Hermann Bitter* (Berlin: 1870; reprint Hildesheim and New York: Olms, 1976), 194: "Sie spielt jede Bach'sche Fuge, aus welcher Tonart man will . . . ."

24. Letter from Schumann to Johann Gottfried Kuntsch, 27 July 1832: "moralisch-stärkende Wirkung auf den ganzen Menschen" (quoted in Klaus-Jürgen Sachs, "Robert Schumanns Fugen über den Namen BACH [op. 60]: Ihr künstlerisches Vorbild und ihr kritischer Maßstab," in *Joh. Seb. Bach und seine Ausstrahlung auf die nachfolgenden Jahrhunderte* [Mainz: Schott, 1980], 151–71). See also the excellent article by Janina Klassen, "Eichenwälder und Blumenwiesen: Aspekte der Rezeption von Bachs 'Wohltemperiertem Klavier' zur Schumann-Zeit," *Archiv für Musikwissenschaft* 53 (1996): 41–64.

25. Karl Storck, "Eine musikalische Hausbibliothek," *Der Türmer* 5 (1902–3): 372–78, at p. 376: "man fange also mit den kleinen Präludien, Phantasien, Inventionen und französischen Suiten an."

process of rationalization, with its description of the piano as a bourgeois piece of furniture—and with its clear love of Bach.[26]

When we finally come to our central concern, namely, reflections of and on Bach in the music of later composers, a vastly different picture emerges—once again demonstrating that the histories of musical ideology, theory, and composition are quite different. Whereas the theoretical and ideological discourse on Bach was dominated by Northern and Middle German authors, and whereas the composers' reactions in the nineteenth century constitute a German chapter of compositional history to such a degree that we can leave out French, Italian, English, Russian, and other reactions (and not only because our time is short), the first chapters were written (as everybody knows) in Vienna. Only on the surface were they linked with the German discussion; they were connected with a specific Habsburgian tradition of counterpoint in church music and instrumental music, as well as with a specific Habsburgian reception not of Bach but Handel.[27]

The connecting link between North Germany and Vienna was (again, as everybody knows) Baron Gottfried van Swieten, who had come to Vienna from Berlin with a lively interest in Handel and Bach and an apparently solid knowledge of both. He is to be credited for creating Austrian interest in Bach, and he promoted the already growing Austrian interest in Handel, an interest sparked by the comparatively widespread transmission of Handel's harpsichord fugues, and an interest that eventually centered on his oratorios, these latter works having come to Vienna from London via Florence.[28] In this pro-

---

26. Max Weber, *Die rationalen und soziologischen Grundlagen der Musik: Mit einer Einleitung von Prof. Dr. Theodor Kroyer* (Munich: Drei Masken Verlag, 1921), 95: "die Stellung eines bürgerlichen 'Möbels', wie dies bei uns schon längst selbstverständlich ist." As for Weber's love of Bach, cf. Christoph Braun, *Max Webers "Musiksoziologie"* (Laaber: Laaber, 1992), esp. 42 ff. See also the critical edition of Max Weber's text in the *Max Weber-Gesamtausgabe*, eds. Ludwig Finscher and Christoph Braun (forthcoming).

27. See Warren Kirkendale, *Fugue and Fugato in Rococo and Classical Chamber Music* (Durham, N.C.: Duke University Press, 1979); Zenck, *Die Bach-Rezeption*; also my own essay, "Bach und die Wiener Klassik" (written in 1975), in *Bachtage Berlin*, ed. Wagner, 139–51; an English version was published as "Bach and the Viennese Classics," *Miscellanea Musicologica: Adelaide Studies in Musicology* 10 (1979): 47–59.

28. Theophil Antonicek, *Zur Pflege Händelscher Musik in der zweiten Hälfte des 18. Jahrhunderts*

cess, the typical differences between North or Middle German and Viennese musical culture emerged once again. As far as we know, it did not provoke theoretical discussion, let alone a discussion with political overtones, and it did not lead to ideological images of Bach or Handel.[29] But it did elicit creative response from the greatest composer in Vienna, something made possible by the sheer coincidence that Van Swieten's Sunday concerts were already in full swing when Mozart settled in the imperial city.

Although Van Swieten was, apart from being a major political figure of his time, a man of many different talents (three of his symphonies even had the honor of being attributed to Haydn), he characteristically made no attempt to infuse his music with elements of Bachian or Handelian counterpoint. Judging from his relatively modest compositional skills, he would scarcely have been able to arrive at a stylistic reorientation via Bach and Handel, even if he tried to do so. On the other hand, quite a number of respectable composers did write in the Austrian church style (heavily fraught not with Bachian or Handelian but Fuxian counterpoint) when necessary, and they did compose instrumental fugues, well aware of the emperor's and his inner circle's strong interest in this kind of music. Mozart could and probably would have done the like. In a letter of 24 March 1781 to his father, he expressed the wish to do so once he was admitted to the emperor: "Well, my main purpose here is to get into the emperor's presence in some becoming way, for I am determined that he shall get to know me. I would love to give him a quick run-through of my opera [*Idomeneo*], and then definitely play fugues, for that is what he likes."[30] But this was a year before Mozart was admitted to the Van Swieten circle. We must assume that he, presumably not knowing any better, would have played "Austrian" fugues for the emperor. But the moment Mozart became acquainted with the Well-Tempered Clavier and the Art of Fugue, he stepped out of the

---

(Vienna: Österreichische Akademie der Wissenschaften, 1966). Cf. also my " '. . . gleichsam ein kanonisirter Tonmeister': Zur deutschen Händel-Rezeption im 18. Jahrhundert," in *Kanon und Zensur: Beiträge zur Archäologie der literarischen Kommunikation II*, ed. Aleida and Jan Assmann (Munich: Fink, 1987), 271–83.

29. Cf. my "Händel und Bach: Zur Geschichte eines musikhistoriographischen Topos," in *Göttinger Händel-Beiträge III* (Kassel: Bärenreiter, 1989), 9–25.

30. *Neue Mozart-Ausgabe: Mozart, Briefe und Aufzeichnungen*, vol. 3 (Kassel: Bärenreiter, 1963), 99.

Austrian tradition. What was significant about this was not so much Mozart's study of Bach and Handel but that he incorporated their elements into his own works—that is, how his style was affected in the process. The important artistic documents are not his arrangements of Bachian fugues, but the great fugal or quasi-fugal compositions of 1782–83 and those that followed: the finale of the G-major string quartet K.387, the first and last movements of the string quartet K.464, the C-minor fugue for two pianos K.426, and so on.

Both before and after (and independent of) Mozart's encounters with Bach's and Handel's music in the early 1780s, there was an established Viennese tradition—though marginal—of copying and arranging Bach fugues: by 1778 Johann Georg Albrechtsberger had copied sixteen fugues from the Well-Tempered Clavier; later came a great number of anonymous arrangements for string ensembles, the forty-eight arrangements by Emanuel Aloys Förster, and of course Beethoven's 1801 and 1817 arrangements of the B♭ minor and B-minor fugues from the first part of the Well-Tempered Clavier. But there were, as far as we know, only a few attempts to write new music in relation to Bach's. A prominent example comes again from Albrechtsberger: his undated fugue on B-A-C-H. Conspicuously, the compositional principle of this work is the exact opposite of Mozart's: it is an attempt at imitation, not adaptation, let alone emulation.

Still more important than the fact that Mozart incorporated elements of Bach and Handel into his own style is the fact that he found a different means of synthesis in each new work. The last movement of the G-major string quartet is a staggeringly complicated and virtuoso combination of sonata and fugue, ancient and modern, Bachian and Austrian counterpoint, modern yet highly personal chromaticism and popular tunefulness. The first and last movements of the A-major quartet involve, even for Mozart, a unique fusion of sonata and freely chromaticized counterpoint. The C-minor fugue for two pianos is a monumental essay in what one could call "dissonant counterpoint," a piece that starts out as a demonstrably archaic fugue but ends with the dissolution of all fugal elements into a modern, thematic coda. There are still other aspects in subsequent works: the solemn and festive counterpoint of the "Jupiter" Symphony, the Bachian chorale setting as one facet of the stylistic universe of *The Magic Flute*, and—a probably unconscious synthesis—the Bachian gigue on a Handelian theme K.574, written in Leipzig in 1789. Time forbids our going more deeply into the matter and citing other examples of this inexhaustable creative fantasy, one that finds ever new ways of developing its own style by adapting Bach's instrumental counterpoint. It is a token, among many, of Mozart's singularity that no subsequent composer found so many ways of infusing an already fully developed personal style with elements of Bachian counterpoint—from the dramatic and symbolic use of a baroque form associated with Bach in K.387's manifest *coincidentia oppositorum* (in which opposite stylistic traits keep their identities), to the chorale setting in *The Magic Flute*, to the different avenues toward complete amalgamation of styles in K.464 and the "Jupiter" Symphony.

There is yet another aspect of Mozart's Bach and Handel reception that has perhaps received too little attention: the differences in functional uses of either Bachian or Handelian elements. As he was for most musicians of the latter eighteenth and the early nineteenth centuries, Bach seems to have been for Mozart a composer of complex, demanding, highly sophisticated instrumental music, whereas Handel was seen as a composer of monumental vocal music tending toward simple and massive effects; Bach a composer for the chamber and for connoisseurs, Handel a composer for the concert hall, the general public, and the representative public occasion. Apparently unique was Mozart's assimilation of both paradigms: there are very few Handelian traits in Mozart's mature instrumental music, but there is a great deal of Handel in the large vocal works, from the C-Minor Mass (with its modeling of the "Qui tollis" on "The people shall hear" from *Israel in Egypt*) to the Requiem (with its borrowings from Handel's *Funeral Anthem for Queen Caroline*, "The ways of Zion do mourn"; and his *Dettingen Anthem*, "The king shall rejoyce" in the Introit and Kyrie).[31] Again, these examples demonstrate quite different ways of dealing with their models: the choir in the C-Minor Mass reflects the idea, the style, and perhaps the poetic imagery of Handel's work without quoting a single measure; the Requiem's Introit takes some thematic ideas, especially the chorale *soggetto*, from Handel's setting and remodels them in a new and origi-

31. The "Qui tollis" was not, as has been so frequently stated, based on the "Crucifixus" of Bach's Mass in B Minor (which Mozart most probably did not know). See Silke Leopold, "Händels Geist in Mozarts Händen: Zum 'Qui tollis' aus der c-Moll-Messe KV 427," *Mozart-Jahrbuch 1994*, 89–111. See the masterly synthesis concerning the Requiem in Christoph Wolff, *Mozarts Requiem: Geschichte, Musik, Dokumente, Partitur des Fragments* (Munich and Kassel: dtv/Bärenreiter, 1991), 75 ff.

nal piece; the Kyrie fugue quotes Handel's two subjects but develops them independently. Maximilian Stadler, so intimately associated with the history of Mozart's Requiem, was the first to discover its connections to Handel's works; likewise, he was the first to suggest that Mozart had studied Handel's music— as he put it—"constantly" and had taken him as his model in composing serious vocal music.[32] Stadler was also one of the first to explain Mozart's mature classical style as a synthesis of influences from Bach, Handel, and Haydn, stating that "in Vienna, in all of Germany, and in all of Europe, he was acknowledged to be the greatest master, someone who had combined Sebastian Bach's art, Handel's strength, and Haydn's most witty clarity and charm."[33]

We know very little about Haydn's relation to Bach, apart from the fact that in his later years he owned Nägeli's edition of the Well-Tempered Clavier together with a manuscript copy of the same work, Breitkopf's edition of the motets, and a manuscript copy of the B-Minor Mass (which he probably acquired from Johann Traeg's copy shop).[34] But there are no traces of Bach in Haydn's music. We can only wonder why this is so. Perhaps the best explanation is that—in his own famous words—"[in the seclusion at Esterhaza] there was nobody . . . to confuse and annoy" him in his creative development, and that by the time he would have had the opportunity to encounter Bach's music, his own style was fully and self-sufficiently developed.[35] It is also worth mentioning that although he knew and played the Well-Tempered Clavier, he had not grown up with it (as his pupil Beethoven had).

Beethoven is a much more difficult case. Fortunately, his relationship with

32. Maximilian Stadler, *Vertheidigung der Echtheit des Mozartischen Requiems* (Vienna, 1826); quoted in Wolff, *Mozarts Requiem*, 149: "Ich fand, wie er unausgesetzt den großen Händel studirte, und ihn zu seinem Muster in ernsthaften Singsachen wählte."

33. Karl Wagner, *Abbé Maximilian Stadler: Seine Materialien zur Geschichte der Musik unter den österreichischen Regenten—Ein Beitrag zum musikalischen Historismus im vormärzlichen Wien* (Kassel: Bärenreiter, 1972), 140: "daß er sowohl in Wienn als ganz Deutschland, in ganz Europa als der größte Meister anerkannt wurde, welcher Sebastian Bachs Kunst, Händels Stärke, Haydns launigste Klarheit und Anmuth in sich verband." See also Zenck, *Die Bach-Rezeption*, 83.

34. Catalogues 1804/05 and 1809; cf. H. C. Robbins Landon, *Haydn: Chronicle and Works*, vol. 5 (London: Thames and Hudson, 1977), 299 ff.

35. Georg August Griesinger, *Biographische Notizen über Josef Haydn* (Leipzig, 1810), 24–25.

Bach has been discussed frequently, and therefore not much need be said here.[36] On the other hand, perhaps we should devote more thought to the fact that there are only faint traces of Bach in Beethoven's early and middle periods, in spite of the fact that he grew up with the Well-Tempered Clavier. Here, as with most later composers, Bach's collection was used as a tool in piano and counterpoint lessons, and although something of its musical essence must have been internalized through the process of learning, apparently an entirely different impulse was necessary for Beethoven—as it was for the later composers—before Bach's music could become an object of creative interest. With Beethoven, this happened most clearly in his late works, beginning around 1815, immediately taking the form of an extremely complicated process of amalgamation on different levels—from more or less obvious imitation of details in the musical language, as for example in parts of op.101, to the fugal style of the opening of the String Quartet in C♯ Minor (a style at once Bachian and extremely modern, pointing well into the future and to *Tristan* and *Ring* polyphony) and the String Quartet in B♭, op.130 (which has recently been interpreted as a gigantic prelude-and-fugue form).[37] In all these inexhaustably rich and enigmatic reconceptions and reworkings of Bach, a kind of double leitmotif seems to emerge: a preoccupation with variation and fugue. This leads us back to the earlier work that appears to represent Beethoven's first creative adaptation of Bachian elements: the "Eroica" Variations, op.35.[38] This was the first widely known set of its time to close and crown a variation cycle with a fugue; and it seems to have been the seminal work in this cyclic form, a form that became so very important in the course of the century—and a form that in itself became closely associated with Bach. The first to follow in Beethoven's footsteps were the variations on a theme of Beethoven by Archduke Rudolph,

36. See above all Zenck, *Die Bach-Rezeption*; see also William Kinderman's essay in the present volume.

37. Barbara R. Barry, "Recycling the End of the 'Leibquartett': Models, Meaning, and Propriety in Beethoven's Quartet in B-Flat Major, opus 130," *Journal of Musicology* 13 (1995): 355–76, esp.363–65.

38. Alexander L. Ringer, "15 Variationen Es-dur für Klavier, 'Eroica-Variationen,' op.35," in *Beethoven: Interpretationen seiner Werke*, vol.1, ed. Albrecht Riethmüller, Carl Dahlhaus, and Alexander L. Ringer (Laaber: Laaber, 1994), 279–89; see also Stefan Kunze, "Die 'wirklich gantz neue Manier' in Beethovens Eroica-Variationen op.35," *Archiv für Musikwissenschaft* 29 (1972): 124–49.

a set that ends with a resounding fugue of enormous dimensions—in every sense, a classical case of intertextuality à la Harold Bloom.[39] In his late works Beethoven, in typically dialectic fashion, at the same time fulfilled and revoked the idea of the apotheosis-like finale fugue: the one is found in the "Hammer-klavier" Sonata, op.106, as well as in the fugue for string quartet op.133, with its fulfillment of Beethoven's ideal of the "poetic" fugue ("tantôt libre, tantôt recherchée"); and the other in the "Diabelli" Variations (which are so closely related to Bach's Goldberg cycle), where Beethoven leads from the apparently finale- and apotheosis-like triple fugue to a finale minuet, one archaic form mirroring and refracting the other (and at the same time opening a subtle dia-logue with Archduke Rudolph's set, which ends with a *tempo di Minuetto* and a fugue).[40] The poetic fugue had already been anticipated to a certain degree in Muzio Clementi's keyboard fugues of 1780/81, and—in a radical fashion that was harshly criticized by Beethoven—in Anton Reicha's thirty-six fugues (published in Vienna, 1803).[41] Here were two more composers who had grown up with the Well-Tempered Clavier.

However venerated and even popular the Viennese Classics were in the

39. Zenck, *Die Bach-Rezeption*, 100–101; see also William Kinderman, *Beethoven's Diabelli Variations* (Oxford: Clarendon Press, 1987), 6, 29.

40. Remark to Karl Holz: "heut zu Tage mus in die alt hergebrachte Form [sc. the fugue] ein anderes, ein wirklich poetisches Element kommen." As for the presence of the "Goldberg" Variations in the "Diabelli" Variations, see Kinderman, *Beethoven Diabelli Variations*, esp.119–20; Martin Zenck, "Rezeption von Geschichte in Beethovens 'Diabelli-Variationen': Zur Ver-mittlung analytischer, ästhetischer und historischer Kategorien," *Archiv für Musikwissenschaft* 37 (1980): 61–75; Zenck, "Bach, der Progressive: Die Goldberg-Variationen in der Perspektive von Beethovens Diabelli-Variationen," in *Musik-Konzepte 42* (Munich, 1985). Cf. Zenck, *Die Bach-Rezeption*, 101; Susan Kagan, *Archduke Rudolph, Beethoven's Patron, Pupil, and Friend: His Life and Music* (Stuyvesant, N.Y.: Pendragon, 1968).

41. Leon Plantinga, *Clementi: His Life and His Music* (London: Oxford University Press, 1977); Anselm Gerhard, *London und der Klassizismus in der Musik: Die Ausprägung einer autonomen Instrumentalmusik in der britischen Musikästhetik des 18. Jahrhunderts und in Muzio Clementis Klavierwerk* (forthcoming). Letter to Breitkopf & Härtel, 18 December 1802: "wie z. B. mir ein gewisser fr. Componist [deleted: "Reicha"] Fugen presentirte apres une nouvelle Methode, welche darin besteht, daß die Fuge keine Fuge mehr ist." See also the rather negative review of Reicha's fugue publication in *Allgemeine musikalische Zeitung* 10, 1807/08, col.353–61. See also Stefan Kunze, "Anton Reichas 'Entwurf einer phrasirten Fuge': Zum Kompositionsbegriff im frühen 19. Jahrhundert," *Archiv für Musikwissenschaft* 25 (1968): 289–307.

early nineteenth century, their Bach reception bore no fruit for the next generation. The most interesting case in point is the young Mendelssohn.[42] The twelve symphonies for strings (1821–23) were student exercises in the classical tradition, even in their fugal movements, turning back especially to Mozart's "Jupiter" Symphony. They do not reflect a conscious attempt at genuine or original Bach reception. As Mendelssohn approached maturity, the situation became much more complicated. In 1827 he worked with three different paradigms simultaneously: the late Beethoven quartets (String Quartet, op.13), the Palestrina tradition (*Tu es Petrus, Te Deum, Hora est*), and Bach (the two fugues from the seven *Charakterstücke*, op.7). But there are traces of Bach in the Palestrinian motets and forebodings of the mature Mendelssohn in the piano fugues. And the string quartet is undoubtedly an original masterpiece: all wrought in one, there is imitation, emulation, and a very demanding sort of intertextuality and originality. Mendelssohn's later development brings clarification through separation of styles (aided by a growing stylistic knowledge of specific genres), and a conversion of the Bach and Beethoven paradigms into a substratum of the now fully developed, highly individual style of the mature composer.

But although Mendelssohn was (as we all know) instrumental in bringing about the celebrated Berlin performances of the St. Matthew Passion, and although he was easily the most influential composer in the generation after Beethoven, the strongest force in Bach reception was not Mendelssohn but Schumann—in his double capacity as composer and highly influential music journalist. Schumann seems to have been the first to formulate clearly a thought that had already marked the Berlin Bach reception around the time of Reichardt and Zelter and that seems to have lurked behind Goethe's famous dictum: Bach's music as something inscrutable and primordial, while Handel seems at once more human and sublime.[43] In exactly the same spirit, Wagner was to compare Bach's music with a prehuman world (see above).

42. Cf. Friedhelm Krummacher, "Bach, Berlin und Mendelssohn: Über Mendelssohns kompositorische Bach-Rezeption," in *Jahrbuch des Staatlichen Instituts für Musikforschung Preußischer Kulturbesitz 1993*, 44–78; cf. also R. Larry Todd, "*Me voila perruqué:* Mendelssohn's Six Preludes and Fugues op.35 reconsidered," in *Mendelssohn Studies*, ed. Todd (Cambridge: Cambridge University Press, 1992), 162–99.

43. "Rückblick auf das Leipziger Musikleben im Winter 1837–1838," in Schumann, *Gesammelte Schriften über Musik und Musiker*, ed. Martin Kreisig (Leipzig: Breitkopf & Härtel, 1914), 376:

Especially in his formative years, Schumann frequently studied and played Bach's music. In March 1838 he wrote to Clara that Bach was "his daily bread," and in the same year he prepared a copy of the Art of Fugue.[44] In 1838 he also composed *Kinderszenen*, *Kreisleriana* (reflecting E. T. A. Hoffmann's Kapellmeister Kreisler, the Bach addict), and *Noveletten*. This marks the beginning of a new stage of Bach reception in composition. Again to Clara, he wrote: "Above all it is strange how I concoct nearly everything as canon but only afterwards discover the imitating voices, frequently even with inversions, retrograde rhythms etc."[45] But as the compositions of 1838 and later show, Bach's influence goes much further and deeper: the whole style of writing is saturated with a Bach experience where the real music has been transformed into a poetic image even before the process of composing has begun. As Georg von Dadelsen put it, the emotional experience and the resulting image are much more important than the real (i.e., technical) influence of the model. Bach's counterpoint has been transformed into poetic counterpoint.[46]

The transformation was so complete that it proves rather difficult to reconstruct the model by analysis, but the influence of Schumann's poetic counterpoint — a kind of meta-Bachian influence — is obvious in Brahms as well as in Wagner. This does not mean, of course, that the two composers did not go beyond Schumann and did not pursue divergent paths in their Bach reception: examples include the specific Brahmsian form of variations and fugue (taken up, made more complicated, and monumentalized by Max Reger), and Wagner's *Meistersinger* prelude, which the composer called "applied Bach" (applied Bach

---

"Über die Bachsche Musik, die gegeben, läßt sich wenig sagen; man muß sie in den Händen haben, studieren möglichst, und er bleibt unergründlich wie vorher. Händel erscheint mir schon menschlich-erhabener."

44. *Jugendbriefe von Robert Schumann*, ed. Clara Schumann (Leipzig: Breitkopf & Härtel, 1885), 279. In the *Musikalische Haus- und Lebensregeln* (Leipzig: Schuberth, 1850), as in the appendix to *Album für die Jugend*, op. 68, edition of 1851, this turned into "Das 'Wohltemperierte Klavier' sei dein täglich Brot. Dann wirst du gewiß ein tüchtiger Musiker."

45. *Jugendbriefe*, 274: "namentlich ist es so sonderbar, wie ich fast alles kanonisch erfinde, und wie ich die nachsingenden Stimmen immer erst hinterdrein entdecke, oft auch in Umkehrungen, verkehrten Rhythmen etc."

46. Georg von Dadelsen, "Robert Schumann und die Musik Bachs," *Archiv für Musikwissenschaft* 14 (1957): 46–59.

it is, but with a vengeance). Wagner's *Tristan* counterpoint had still been firmly rooted in Schumann's poetic adaptation of Bach. His *Meistersinger* counterpoint is differentiated into a highly complex system: counterpoint as craft, parodistic counterpoint, and meditative or affective (emotional) counterpoint. At the same time, one can view this system as an unfolding of the potential embodied in creative Bach reception after Schumann.[47] In its turn, Wagner's *Meistersinger* counterpoint has deeply influenced even those composers who had no direct and intimate dealings with Bach's music—we have only to think of Strauss's *Also sprach Zarathustra* or *Sinfonia domestica*.

If what I have sketched so far can be understood as a more or less one-directional process arising with the second wave in Bach reception (Mendelssohn and Schumann), a quite different situation develops around and after the turn of the century—now no longer a gradual progression but a constellation of bewildering complexity. Perhaps this is a direct outcome of the general situation around 1900, characterized by a multiplicity of styles and tendencies as well as by general feelings of insecurity and disorientation. This time marks the virtual end of tonality in art music on the one hand, and on the other (since contemporary music became more and more difficult to play and to understand) a steadily expanding market for "early" repertory in music publishing and concert life. It also marks the completion of the Bach-Ausgabe and various activities of the Neue Bach-Gesellschaft that were aimed at making Bach a popular composer in public and private musical life. Ever since the last *contrapunctus* of the Art of Fugue, there had been compositions on Bach's name, but now they began to abound. There had been a wide spectrum of stylistic means to absorb Bach's music, but now the whole gamut, from the simple quotation of the name B–A–C–H to the most sophisticated techniques of stylistic integration, was being explored. At the same time, these very techniques of integration became more refined the more the spectrum of stylistic and technical possibilities grew. This situation became possible the more Bach's music was seen as meta-historical on the one hand, while on the other hand historical consciousness was growing and the process of, and especially the teaching of, composition was increasingly historicized.

47. Cf. my "Über den Kontrapunkt der 'Meistersinger' ", in *Das Drama Richard Wagners als musikalisches Kunstwerk*, ed. Carl Dahlhaus (Regensburg: Gustav Bosse, 1970), 303–12; Werner Breig, "Wagners kompositorisches Werk," in *Richard-Wagner-Handbuch*, ed. Ulrich Müller and Peter Wapnewski (Stuttgart: Alfred Kröner, 1986), 353–470, esp. 450–51.

It may be sufficient to name the two composers who around and shortly after the turn of the century were most deeply involved in the problem of coming to terms with Bach and who, prior to Schoenberg, Berg, and Webern, found the most original and radical answers: Max Reger and Ferruccio Busoni.

The case of Reger is especially complicated because he—much more consistently than any earlier composer—wrote music at different levels of complexity and in different grades of approximation to Bach, all the while never renouncing the claim of producing artworks of the highest order.[48] His whole output is saturated by contrapuntal thinking, but there is a clear distinction between forms and genres coming from the Viennese classics via Brahms (symphonic pieces and solo concertos or overtures) and those coming from Bach (chorale cantatas, solo sonatas, and most of the organ music).

There is a further distinction within the latter group. Reger's large, mostly hypertrophied organ works are a curious and nearly unique blend of neo-Bachian counterpoint, Bach allusions, and an excessively chromatic harmonic language just bordering on atonality—a style prefigured only in some of Liszt's organ works and in the monumental organ sonata of Julius Reubke. The style of Reger's chorale cantatas is radically different. These are small, unpretentious works which, with quite subtle means, reflect an attempt to transform the Bachian cantata type, which at the time (around 1900) was considered the most advanced and venerable type, into decidedly modern music; in addition, he aimed in these works to reconcile Protestant worship and contemporary music. The cantatas show, in other words, Reger's effort to become a modern Thomas-Cantor, just as in his organ works he had aspired to become a modern Thomas-Organist. Different again are the solo pieces for violin, viola, or violoncello. Whereas the early sonatas of op. 42 and 91 are comparatively close to Bach and are much less complicated or modern than the chamber music of the same years, the preludes and fugues of op. 117 and op. 131a are much more

---

48. Only the most recent and most important titles can be listed here: Lorenzen, *Max Reger als Bearbeiter Bachs*; Roman Brotbeck, *Zum Spätwerk von Max Reger: Fünf Diskurse* (Wiesbaden: Breitkopf & Härtel, 1988); Friedhelm Krummacher, "Zwischen Avantgarde und Konvention: Regers Kammermusik in der Gattungsgeschichte," in *Reger-Studien 4*, ed. Susanne Shigihara (Wiesbaden: Breitkopf & Härtel, 1989), 193–217; Friedhelm Krummacher "Auseinandersetzung im Abstand: Über Regers Verhältnis zu Bach," in *Reger-Studien 5*, ed. Susanne Shigihara (Wiesbaden: Breitkopf & Härtel, 1993), 11–39. See also Walter Frisch's essay in the present volume.

modern, especially in their harmonic language. They also—more important—
feature not general and atmospheric quasi-Bachian language but demonstrably
Bachian fugal subjects or even subjects from specific Bach works (as in op.117,
no.5, for example). In both cases, the subjects undergo thoroughly modern
chromatic treatment, so that the points of departure and arrival in each work,
so to speak, span the whole compositional development from the early eighteenth to the early twentieth centuries. Or to put it more aptly: Regers's is a
kind of music that no longer aims, as earlier Bach reception had done, either at
imitation or stylistic synthesis but rather toys with the *coincidentia oppositorum*.
The procedure is not far from Busoni's *Fantasia contrappuntistica*. Similarly,
Busoni's second violin sonata of 1898, the spiritual and architectonic center of
which is a Bach chorale that becomes the theme for a set of variations, points
to the Bach chorale in Alban Berg's violin concerto.[49]

Taking everything together and allowing for some inevitable oversimplifi-
cation, it should not be difficult to arrive at a typology. At one end of the spectrum stand the arrangements of which I have not spoken: the late romantic
and post-romantic ones scored for the instrumental combinations and forces
of their time (Busoni, Schoenberg, Stokowski, and Robert Franz) and the analytical ones that can turn into great works of art of their own kind (Webern).
The next step is the quotation of or composition on the name B–A–C–H, a
secular—or perhaps not quite secular—rite that seems to be connected, at least
subconsciously, with the ritual pronouncement of the name of a divine being.
Obviously the B–A–C–H subject can serve well in quite different stylistic en-
vironments and at quite different levels of sophistication and craftsmanship,
from the unassuming fugue by Albrechtsberger to the fugues and fantasias of
Liszt, Reger, and Busoni. Logically the next step, but technically altogether a
different matter, is quotation from Bach's actual compositions, which one encounters, for example, in Busoni's violin sonata and Berg's violin concerto.
This is a technique that could work only in a time of highest stylistic refinement and historical consciousness. A still further step is the free fantasy upon a
specific work or group of works by Bach (as opposed to the simpler and usually
not very interesting fantasy upon a Bach theme), which, again, requires a certain level of refinement and a late stage of development; here Busoni's *Fantasia*

49. Albrecht Riethmüller, "Bach in Busonis 2. Violinsonate," in *Jahrbuch des Staatlichen Instituts
für Musikforschung Preußischer Kulturbesitz 1995*, 51–65.

*after Bach* of 1909 and the *Fantasia contrappuntistica* (four versions 1910/1922) come to mind, pieces the composer called "Nachdichtungen" (poetic paraphrases). The few significant and many insignificant cycles of preludes and fugues modeled on the Well-Tempered Clavier represent an extreme point, where surface relations to Bach's music have been reduced to a minimum while spiritual ones are still very strong. The most significant of these cycles include Chopin's preludes of 1836/39, Shostakovich's preludes and fugues of 1950/51, and Hindemith's *Ludus tonalis* of 1942.

In a different sequence, one could arrange the historical evidence according to stylistic criteria. Here the line would lead from conscious attempts at imitation (e.g., some of the fugue fragments by Mozart and the two fugues from Mendelssohn's op.7). It would move on to intermediate stages of juxtaposition or style quotation in a stylistically foreign context (again, Mozart к.387), then to amalgamation and synthesis (once again Mozart, the "Jupiter" Symphony and the overture to *The Magic Flute*). And what seem to be final stages of the development would involve three types of transformation: fugue that is derived from Bach is still a fugue, but it is stylistically completely unrelated to his music (Beethoven, *Grosse Fuge* op.133); counterpoint that is derived from Bach but is something new and for its time quite modern, with no remaining traces of the Bach idiom (Mozart, к.464); and music that is not even contrapuntal in the traditional sense but is in some mysterious, poetic way quite close to Bach (Schumann).

But beyond all factual evidence and all typologies, the most important point is rather simple: there is no composer other than Bach who has had such an influence on his colleagues, in so many different ways, and over such a long stretch of time—at least until the end of compositional history in the traditional, Eurocentric sense (i.e., the death of Anton von Webern in 1945). There is no composer who has written music history so long after his death. It is time to begin to reconstruct this history.

# Bach among
# the Theorists

## Thomas Christensen

One of the most striking ironies about Bach's musical legacy to the second half of the eighteenth century was the number of theoretically active students he bequeathed. For one who was supposedly uninterested in—not to say antipathetic to—matters of speculative music theory, Bach taught a surprisingly large number of pupils who went on to publish important theoretical and pedagogical works: Johann Philipp Kirnberger, Christoph Nichelmann, Lorenz Mizler, Johann Friedrich Agricola, Johann Christian Kittel, and of course his own son, Carl Philipp Emanuel Bach. Indeed, it is hard to think of any other composer to this day who has produced such a bevy of loquacious music pedants.[1] And if we widen the circle a bit, we can identify still more theorists who, although not direct students of Bach, nonetheless claimed some degree of filiation to his musical circle or otherwise strongly identifed themselves with his legacy. Such "associative" pupils of Bach include Wilhelm Friedrich Marpurg, Ernst Friedrich Wolf, Christoph Gottlieb Schröter, Christian Reichardt, Johann A. P. Schulz, and August F. C. Kollmann.

For their helpful suggestions and critical comments on an earlier version of this paper, I would like to thank David Schulenberg, Daniel Melamed, and Jeanne Swack. Special gratitude is owed to my colleague and fellow Bach enthusiast Delbert Disselhorst, to whom, in celebration of twenty-five years of inspirational teaching and performing on the organ at the University of Iowa, I respectfully dedicate this essay.

1. One candidate who does come to mind was a cousin of Sebastian: Johann Nicolaus Bach. The "Jena" Bach was a famous pedagogue whose pupils included several important theorists of the early eighteenth century, including Friedrich Erhard Niedt, Johann Philipp Treiber, Johann Georg Neidhardt, and Christoph Gottlieb Schröter. For a discussion of Nicolaus Bach's theory pedagogy, see my article "Johann Nikolaus Bach als Musiktheoretiker," *Bach-Jahrbuch* 82 (1996): 93–100.

There are certainly good reasons to doubt that Bach himself would have encouraged any scholarly inclinations among his students. Mizler put it mildly
when he lamented in 1751 that "our late departed Bach did not, it is true, occupy
himself with deep theoretical or speculative matters in music," consoling himself that Bach thereby "was all the stronger in the practice of the art."[2] Taking
a more dogmatic stance, Carl Philipp Emanuel told Forkel emphatically that
his father "like myself or any true musician was no lover of dry mathematical
stuff."[3] Scheibe, who we know was certainly not hesitant to criticize any defi-
ciencies he might discern in Bach's music, nonetheless strongly defended Bach
from the charge of being a composer who could be incriminated by any association with mathematically based *musica theoria*.[4]

Indeed, there is no evidence to suggest Bach was ever interested in speculative music theory, despite his having joined Mizler's musical society in 1747, an
organization dedicated precisely to the kinds of abstract theorizing so scorned
by Philipp Emanuel.[5] The only documents we know from Bach's atelier that
could be at all classified as theoretical are some notes on realizing a figured
bass: "Vorschriften und Grundsätze zum vierstimmigen spielen des General-
Bass oder Accompagnement."[6]

But as Spitta long ago recognized, these "Precepts" are largely cribbed passages from the first nine chapters of Friederich Niedt's *Die Musicalische Handleitung* (Hamburg, 1700), with supplementary illustrations and exercises provided as an addendum.[7] It is not clear how firmly these notes and supplements

2. BR, 278.

3. BR, 278.

4. BDOK 2, no. 468.

5. Bach's own library contained a modest number of theory texts, including Fux's *Gradus*. And
we know too that Bach acted as a sales agent for several theoretical works, including the lexicon
by his cousin Walther, as well as Johann Heinichen's mammoth treatise, *Der General-Bass in der
Composition*. None of this seems surprising, though, given Bach's long residency in Leipzig—
one of the major centers of the book trade in Germany at the time. The point is not that Bach
was unaware of theoretical writings in his day—it would have been incredible given his prominent music positions and activities as a teacher had he somehow remained ignorant of them.
Rather, it is that none of these theoretical writings seems to have had a discernible impact.

6. Translated by Pamela Poulin as *Precepts and Principles for Playing the Thorough Bass or Accom-
panying in Four Parts* (Oxford: Clarendon Press, 1994).

7. Philip Spitta, "Bachiana: Der Tractat über den Generalbass und F. Niedt's 'Musikalische
Handleitung,'" *Musikgeschichtliche Aufsätze* (Berlin, 1894), 121–28.

can be tied to Bach.[8] In any event, there is little in them that bespeaks any intellectual interest in music theory beyond rendering a practical, condensed pedagogical guide to the realization of figured-bass signatures.

To be sure, Bach was an active teacher of keyboard and composition.[9] Yet as a pedagogue, Bach had an approach that seems to have been purely empirical, one that owed little to the methods or theories of any of his predecessors (with the possible exception of Niedt). C. P. E. Bach accounted for this by the simple explanation that, "since he himself had composed the most instructive pieces for the clavier, he brought up his pupils on them."[10] From everything we know, J. S. Bach's "theory" was entirely applied and dispensed with contemporary strategies—to offer four representative examples—for organizing and explaining figured-bass signatures using varieties of inversional theory (as employed, for example, by Heinichen, Sorge, Kellner), classifying types of fugal subject and answer (Mattheson, Walther), systematically laying down principles of dissonance employment in simple counterpoint (Fux, Scheibe), or calculating the interval ratios of various kinds of mean-tone temperaments (Neidhardt, Sinn, Sorge).[11] Still less is there any evidence of the kinds of speculative or

8. See the discussion by Hans-Joachim Schulze in *Studien zur Bach Überlieferung im 18. Jahrhundert* (Leipzig: Edition Peters, 1984), 125-27. Schulze identifies the Bach student Carl August Thieme as the scribe for at least the title page and certain emendations to the text.

9. Most of the relevant evidence is collected and discussed in the informative article by David Schulenberg, "Composition and Improvisation in the School of J. S. Bach," in *Bach Perspectives 1*, ed. Russell Stinson (Lincoln: University of Nebraska Press, 1995), 1–42.

10. BR, 279.

11. Alfred Dürr has suggested that a series of quasi-figured-bass analytic notations on several Bach manuscripts might represent the theoretical teachings of the Master ("Ein Dokument aus dem Unterricht Bachs?" *Musiktheorie* 1 [1987]: 163-70). Dürr discusses three movements from Well-Tempered Clavier I—the fugues in C minor and B minor, and the prelude in D minor—found in Mus. ms. Bach P 401. (Similar analytic markings not noted in Dürr's article can be found in the Sarabande and two Menuets from the French Suite in D Minor, BWV 812 in P 418.) It is hard to imagine, though, in what way these fussy, mechanical markings could represent the teachings of Bach, or what insight into the music they offer. The "analysis," such as it is, consists of the scale degree identification of the lowest voice (coupled with frequent mode changes) against which all the other voices are intervallically measured. As Heinrich Deppert pointed out in a follow-up letter to Dürr's article, many of these analytic markings are incorrect and undoubtedly represent the additions of some later—and unsophisticated—music student (Heinrich Deppert, "Anmerkungen zu Alfred Dürr," *Musiktheorie* 2 [1988]: 107-8).

abstract theorizing found in the writings of Werckmeister, Murschauser, or Fuhrmann.[12]

Whatever indifference Bach may have evinced when it came to matters of music theory, it did not stop any of his opinionated disciples from calling upon his authority when it came to staking their own points of view. Over and over we find Bach's name and music drawn into heated polemics during the eighteenth century in order to support the widest spectrum of theoretical positions—and often by opposing sides. Bach's name became something of a rhetorical talisman to these theorists, cited with the same piety as was Newton's by English philosophers in their battles over sensationalist epistemology and latitudinarianism.

For all their pedantry and penchant for polemic, these theorists deserve credit for the maintenance of Bach's music in the second half of the eighteenth century. In fact, virtually every published citation or discussion of Bach's music between the appearance of the Art of Fugue in 1752 and the first edition of the Well-Tempered Clavier in 1801 occurred in a theory treatise or article—and, more typically than not, in the context of some theoretical dispute. Even the appearance of Bach's chorales in the editions of Birnstiel and Kirnberger—the only autonomous publications of Bach's music in this period—was part of a pedagogical agenda rooted in an ongoing argument, one with important theoretical implications, as we will see.

The contributions of these theorists go beyond custodial roles, though; their writings reveal the real enigma Bach the man posed after midcentury, and the difficulty in interpreting the significance of his compositional legacy. Having written almost nothing but a few aphoristic comments concerning his views on music to guide them, it remained for theorists to interpret Bach for themselves. Yet this proved to be not an easy task, for Bach seemed to be many things to each observer. It was possible to find something in his compositions to justify nearly any point of view.

Perhaps the most dramatic illustration of this situation can be seen in the re-

12. Jan Chiapusso is representative of those twentieth-century writers who have tried to paint a picture of Bach as a hermetic music theorist, one who clandestinely studied speculative music theorists like Kepler and Werckmeister in addition to the cabalistic divinations of the Pythagoreans, Neoplatonists, and asundry Christian mystics (Chiapusso, *Bach's World* [Bloomington: Indiana University Press, 1968]). Such a picture, however, is wildly overdrawn and is itself a product of the most extravagant speculation.

spective positions of Lorenz Mizler and Johann Mattheson. No two individuals seemed to represent more opposing world views than did these—Mizler, the parochial, academic schoolmaster possessing unbounded faith in the power of mathematics and reason to unlock the mysteries of music; and Mattheson, the blustery, vain, and worldly music critic, possessing an equally adamant empirical and pragmatic view of music. For Mizler, the heir to the great tradition of ancient harmonic theory, music represented a venerable science of number and cosmic truth, one demanding of the pious observer deep philosophical contemplation and diligent, rational analysis. It was of course for just this purpose that he founded his "Korrespondierende Sozietät der Musicalischen Wissenschaften."[13]

For Mattheson, the numerical mysticism and rationalist jargon spouted by Mizler and his society represented just the kind of nonsense he had been campaigning against since his very first publications. Music must always be judged by the ear, not the mind, Mattheson would continually reprove. Mathematics has as little to do with understanding music as does hydraulics with sailing.[14] Such an empirical bias, naturally, was anathema to Mizler. He felt that the unreflective criticism of Mattheson doomed music to the function of mere entertainment and licentious epicurianism, rather than providing the profound spiritual and ethical edification of which it was capable.

Yet both authors saw Bach as an ally to their respective positions. For Mizler, Bach was the learned master of double counterpoint and harmony, whose intricate compositions both challenged and vindicated the careful, disciplined kinds of mathematical investigation to which Mizler dedicated his society.[15] Mattheson saw Bach in a completely different light: as the sober church Kan-

---

13. BR, 440.

14. I have analyzed Matteson's complex empiricism in some detail in my article "*Sensus, Ratio, and Phthongos:* Mattheson's Theory of Tone Perception," in *Musical Transformation and Musical Intuition*, ed. Raphael Atlas and Michael Cherlin (Roxbury: Ovenbird Press, 1994), 1–22.

15. Christoph Schröter, who often served as Mizler's advocate, was perhaps an even stronger proponent of this viewpoint. In a spirited rebuttal to the skeptical attacks of Scheibe and Mattheson on Mizler's work (incidentally in the same article in which he summarized the Scheibe/Birnbaum controversy [BDOK 2, no. 552]), Schröter offers a resounding defense of scientific music theory and its value to musicians—implicitly drawing Bach in as an ally in the context of Scheibe's attacks. See "Die Notwendigkeit der Mathematik bey gründlicher Erlehrung der musikalischen Composition," *Musicalischer Bibliothek*, III/2 (Leipzig, 1746).

tor, virtuosic organist, and diligent *Musikant* who had neither the time nor need for the kinds of sterile speculations and abstractions of Mizler.[16] Compounding the irony, both men cited similar works of Bach for their positions: Mizler hailed the canonic variations *Vom Himmel hoch*—the work, we will recall, Bach submitted to Mizler's society upon his joining in 1747—as the most profound example of musical science.[17] Yet Mattheson could cite just five years later the Art of Fugue as symbolizing a quite different achievement: the culmination of a venerable German compositional genre by its most talented and industrious practitioner.[18]

To be sure, it is easy to overdraw these polarities. Neither Mizler nor Mattheson can be accused of constancy when it came to their opinions. Mizler, after all, composed some of the most pedestrian odes in the galant style published in the eighteenth century, while Mattheson was capable of writing extended Pietistic reveries about music's ethical and spiritual powers, not to mention some astoundingly convoluted academic counterpoint of his own.[19] Nor were Mizler and Mattheson necessarily always at odds. As a student in Leipzig, Mizler saw fit to dedicate his profoundly scholastic music dissertation of 1731

16. BR, 440.

17. Properly speaking, it was a six-voice canon (BWV 1076) that Bach first submitted to Mizler's society in 1747 (BDOK 3, no. 665). The "Vom Himmel hoch" canons came afterwards as a kind of dedicatory commission upon his initiation to the society (BR, 224). Another writer who praised the canonic variations in similar terms was the theologian Johann Michael Schmidt. In his *Musico-Theologia, oder erbauliche Anwendung musicalisher Wahrheiten* (Bayreuth, 1754), a quaint treatise that attempts to amalgamate theology and music theory (arguing, for example, that the triadic partials of the harmonic overtone series are a demonstration of the Christian Trinity [p.123]), Schmidt claims that the most complex geometrical proofs and the most profound and painstaking reflection put together could not come close to equaling the thought that Bach put into this music (p.150, cited in BDOK 3, no. 659). Elsewhere, Schmidt hails Bach's "final" chorale, *Wenn wir in höchsten Nöthen Seyn*, as a devastating blow to the advocates of materialism (p.197).

18. BDOK 3, no. 647.

19. Lorenz Mizler, *Sammlungen auserlesener moralischer Oden*, 3 vols. (Leipzig, 1740–42); facsimile, ed. Dragan Plamenac (Leipzig: Deutscher Verlag für Musik, 1972). Johann Mattheson, *Die wohlklingende Fingersprache* (Hamburg, 1735). For Mattheson's music theology, see my article "*Sensus, Ratio*, and *Phthongos*," 12–14.

to both Mattheson and Bach.[20] And Mizler promoted and excerpted many of Mattheson's writings in his journal.[21]

Still, the essential positions of Mizler and Mattheson on questions of *musica speculativa* do capture a familiar tension in Bach's music. As a composer, Bach could be both sublime and worldly; his astonishing varieties of music seem to run the gamut from the profoundly rational to the profanely practical. It is not hard to see how Mizler and Mattheson found confirmation for their respective views when they turned to his music.

However, it was not just rarified ontological questions about music and its speculative grounding into which Bach's music was drawn. Pressing concerns about changing musical styles were also at issue. As a response to this, Christoph Nichelmann issued his spirited critique of galant stylisms and aesthetics, boldly claiming for support the music of J. S. Bach.[22] By demonstrating how the harmonic richness evinced in the best of Bach's music enhanced and supported all his melodies, Nichelmann hoped to resolve the smoldering debate over the relative merits of harmony and melody recently ignited in France by Rousseau and Rameau.[23] As seen in example 1, Nichelmann revealed the harmonic richness of Bach's music by invoking an analytic tool newly arrived in Germany: Rameau's fundamental bass. In the analysis of the E-Major Sarabande, BWV 817/3, the bottom system shows the idealized harmonic structure that he claims underlies its melodic realization in the top system. Despite the fact that he understood Rameau's theory imperfectly, Nichelmann's analysis makes two important claims about Bach's music, one not at all controversial, the other decidedly so. First, Bach's compositional art could be seen as a *har-*

20. BDOK 2, no. 349. However, it cannot be ruled out that this dedication was more a calculated political move on Mizler's part than any reflection of real intellectual affinity.

21. To underscore the precariousness of any facile demarcations when it comes to eighteenth-century music theory, let it be noted that Scheibe, when he otherwise was not criticizing writers like Mizler for their learned academicisms, found time to write a treatise on interval generation and classification that was as abstract and pedantic as any written in the entire century: *Eine Abhandlung von den musicalischen Intervallen und Geschlechten* (Hamburg, 1739).

22. *Die Melodie nach ihrem Wesen sowohl, als nach ihren Eigenschaften* (Danzig, 1755), 59–61.

23. It should perhaps be mentioned that even Bach could come into criticism by Nichelmann for occasional lapses in good taste: see the critique of BWV 84/1 found on p. 129 (and cited in BDOK 3, no. 668).

EX.1. Christoph Nichelmann's fundamental-bass analysis of BWV 817
(from Nichelmann, *Die Melodie*, 1755)

*monic* achievement. This, as we will soon see, was a widely accepted proposition among musicians in the eighteenth century. It was Nichelmann's second claim that in fact was the most incendiary: that this harmonic practice could be best explained using an analytic theory imported from France.

Of course it was Friedrich Wilhelm Marpurg—the prolific journalist and critic on the River Spree—who claimed to be Rameau's faithful exegete in Germany. And for better or worse, it was Marpurg who was responsible for presenting Rameau's theories in Germany during the 1750s, even though Marpurg's interpretation, like Nichelmann's, was flawed.[24] At the same time, Marpurg also believed himself to be a faithful partisan of Bach's compositional legacy. While Marpurg never enjoyed formal tutelage with the Master himself, he claimed to have discussed musical issues with Bach on numerous occasions and to have enjoyed his confidence.[25] It was Marpurg, after all, who aided C. P. E. Bach in the publication of the Art of Fugue—and for whose second edition he provided a preface.[26] Most critically, it was Marpurg who published two years later the most detailed study of the tonal fugue to appear in Germany during the eighteenth century—the *Abhandlung von der Fuge* (Berlin, 1753). Marpurg saw the fugue as salutary for composers at midcentury, a genre that could help clear away, as he put it, "the spreading rubbish of effeminate song" then plaguing Germany.[27] Again, it would be too much to demand of Marpurg consistency in practice, since he composed and promoted in his journals the very kind of lightweight minuettes, marches, and odes that have given the galant such a malodorous name. His few attempts at fugal writing—as with Mattheson—are so inept and academically stilted that it is a wonder historians have not treated the *Abhandlung* with a bit more circumspection and skepticism.

Still, Marpurg's attempt to rehabilitate the fugue along Bachian lines was unlikely to succeed. For most composers in the second half of the eighteenth century, the fugue was an antiquated, if venerable, genre.[28] What fugal pedagogy there was consisted of revisions within the paradigm of Fuxian strict counterpoint.[29] Bach's fugal art, while selectively appreciated by a few connoisseurs (such as Kirnberger's pupil Princess Anna Amalia and Mozart's patron,

---

24. Joel Lester, *Compositional Theory in the Eighteenth Century* (Cambridge, Mass.: Harvard University Press, 1992), 233–39.

25. BR, 257.

26. BDOK 3, no. 648.

27. BR, 268.

28. Imogene Horsley, *Fugue: History and Practice* (New York: Free Press, 1966), 261.

29. This would include the treatises of Paolucci, Martini, Azopardi, Albrechtsberger, Sabbatini, Choron, and Langlé—the latter two writers being largely responsible for the establishment in France of the notorious nineteenth-century tradition of the conservatory fugue (*fugue d'école*). Alfred Mann, *The Study of Fugue* (New Brunswick, N.J.: Rutgers University Press, 1958), 57–61.

van Swieten), was hardly seen as a viable compositional model.[30] The issue, though, was really not one of genre cultivation—that is, whether the fugue (or for that matter, the canon or chorale) was still a vital genre to composers after midcentury. Clearly, given the popular musical tastes of the day, this could not be. The challenge posed by Bach's music was a different one, touching on a broader conception of compositional theory and pedagogy. Put simply: Was there some common compositional basis that underlay all of Bach's music regardless of style or genre? And could this basis be identified and explicated by theorists in such a way as to have value for contemporaneous composers?

For Johann Philipp Kirnberger, such a common structural basis existed in *Reiner Satz*—pure four-part composition. All of Bach's music, Kirnberger believed, was structured by the model of four-part harmony, regardless of the particular *Schreibart* or *Gattung*. It was precisely to elucidate and codify this harmonic underpinning that Kirnberger wrote his monumental *Die Kunst des reinen Satzes*, claiming that it faithfully reflected Bach's own pedagogy of composition.[31] On this point, we do have some rare corroborating testimony. C. P. E. Bach confirmed to Forkel that his father would begin with the harmonization of figured basses and chorale melodies when instructing his students, and only then move on to two- and three-part textures and the fugue: "His pupils had to begin their studies by learning pure four-part thorough bass. From this he went to chorales; first he added the basses to them himself, and they had to invent the alto and tenor. Then he taught them to devise the basses themselves. He particularly insisted on the writing out of the thorough bass in [four real] parts."[32]

In our own pedagogical tradition, in which harmony and counterpoint are strongly demarcated (Schenkerian theory notwithstanding), Kirnberger's identification of Bach as harmonist might strike us as odd. But it was hardly considered so in the eighteenth century. When critics and theorists in Bach's day praised his music, it was almost always in terms of harmony, not con-

---

30. The only theory treatise after Marpurg in the eighteenth century that to any degree attempts to take account of Bach's fugal art was penned by A. F. C. Kollmann, a follower of Kirnberger: *An Essay on Practical Musical Composition* (London, 1799); BDOK 3, no.1021.

31. BDOK 3, no.861.

32. BR, 279.

trapuntal texture or the genre of the fugue. Reichardt thought Bach to have been the "greatest harmonist of all time and of all people," while Marpurg thought the virtue of Bach's Art of Fugue was precisely its potential to restore the "dignity of harmony."[33] Of course, when these theorists made reference to harmony, few of them were thinking exclusively of vertical chords or their succession. The exigencies of dissonance treatment and the need to create and sustain flowing, independent voices to shape chords—today we would call it voice-leading—was an indispensable element in all harmonic pedagogy. Still, there was an indisputable chordal element to these theorists' views on harmony that should not be obscured on account of any twentieth-century ideology. Nichelmann's commentary on the first eight measures of BWV 817 reproduced in example 1 illustrates well this harmonic prejudice: "Within a period of just eight measures, this composition not only displays a sufficient quantity and variety of chords such that the most natural desires of the soul are satisfied by a sufficient diversity of harmony, thereby fulfilling the primary and most universal function of music, but these differing harmonies are also ideally suited to the specific nature of the music."[34]

Over and over we find eighteenth-century critics singling out Bach's astonishing harmonic inventiveness as his crowning compositional legacy.[35] To place emphasis upon Bach's harmonic inventiveness at the expense of his contrapuntal mastery would in no way lessen his image as a "learned" composer. Nor was Bach's harmonic art seen in any way less susceptible to pedagogical study and emulation. This is surely the reason that, of all of Bach's many compositions awaiting publication in the later eighteenth century, it was his four-part chorales that were issued first. Kirnberger's determination—one might better say, obsession—to see the chorales published in his lifetime was driven by his

---

33. BDOK 3, no. 853; BR, 268.

34. *Die Melodie*, 59.

35. Harmony, it is also important to keep in mind, was viewed as no less of a demanding and learned science in the eighteenth century than was counterpoint, and consequently no less susceptible to the kinds of academic systematization and pedagogy we tend to associate with strict counterpoint. Music theorists like Marpurg, Schröter, and Friedrich Riedt produced lengthy texts that exhaustively attempted to generate and classify chords. Their writings were rigidly quantitative and rationally abstract enough to make even the most orthodox Cartesian blush. (See, for example, Riedt's tables and analysis of "all" possible three- and four-note chords in Marpurg's *Historische und Kritische Beiträge zur Musik*, II, 5 [1756], 387–413.)

conviction that they represented the richest pedagogical models of harmonic art ever conceived. And it also explains the horror and sense of ethical betrayal Kirnberger and C. P. E. Bach expressed at the appearance of Birnstiel's corrupt edition of the chorales.[36]

Throughout the eighteenth century, it was Bach's chorales that received the most attention and praise from theorists, not his instrumental music or larger vocal pieces.[37] Early on, theorists recognized—as they do today—that Bach's chorales offer an unparalleled compendium of harmonic vocabulary and voicing with inexhaustible pedagogical value. Agricola—who at one point was asked by Kirnberger to help edit the chorales—marveled with "what art and harmonic genius" these chorales were composed. "While his melodies may not be as charming and touching as others, they are all controlled by the richest harmonies in such a natural and unconstrained manner, one would break into quite a sweat trying to write something of their equal."[38] In 1785, Schulz thought that the chorales might constitute by themselves an "enduring handbook of practical harmony."[39]

Not all theorists were unanimous in endorsing Bach's chorales, however. Johann Christoph Kuhnau, a student of Kirnberger's, admitted that Bach's four-part chorales were great pedagogical models, but he thought that they worked poorly as actual hymns to be sung in church.[40] The Abbé Vogler was an even stronger critic, believing Bach's chorales to be filled with crude part writing, obscure modal identities, and gross violations of harmonic syntax. (Vogler claimed to rectify these "problems" in his own notorious recomposition [*Verbesserung*] of a dozen of Bach's chorales.)[41] But Vogler's opinion was really the exception, as was made plain by the deluge of ridicule and sarcasm that rained

36. The story is related in BR, 270–74.

37. See the representative comments of Marpurg (BDOK 3, no. 702), Reichardt (no. 845), Knecht (no. 990), and Forkel (no. 1048).

38. BDOK 3, no. 733.

39. BDOK 3, no. 906.

40. BDOK 3, no. 898.

41. BDOK 3, nos. 1013–14, 1017, and 1039. For an illustration and balanced discussion of Vogler's "improvements," see Floyd K. Grave and Magaret G. Grave, *In Praise of Harmony: The Teaching of Abbé Georg Vogler* (Lincoln: University of Nebraska Press, 1987), 167–71.

down upon his *Choral System*. For virtually every other observer in the second half of the eighteenth century, Bach's chorales were models of harmonic pedagogy to be studied and emulated.[42]

Kirnberger was keen to show that the same harmonic logic that is so perfectly manifested in the four-part chorale in fact underlies all of Bach's music. To do this, he began with the received practice of the thorough bass. According to Bach's well-known definition (borrowed from Niedt), the thorough bass was the "most perfect foundation of music . . . [resulting in] a full-sounding *Harmonie* to the Honour of God and the permissible delight of the soul."[43] Extrapolating from this, Kirnberger deduced that *all* music is derived from four-part harmonic backgrounds that could be elucidated through the thorough bass.[44] But Kirnberger wanted to go one step further and show how this harmonic background within the thorough bass was itself reducible to an even more simplified construction. And this is where Rameau's fundamental bass proved so useful. It was not so much the generative elements of Rameau's theory that was of interest to Kirnberger, as it was to Marpurg; rather, it was the reductive element. Rameau's theory proved uniquely suited to showing how all tonal music could be reduced to a small number of logically related harmonic entities whose succession was controlled by an underlying fundamental bass.[45] It is certainly true that Kirnberger was no slavish disciple of Rameau. Indeed, for various political reasons to be discussed later, he tried to distance

42. Within a few years after their publication (in 1784), a number of theorists did indeed fulfill Kirnberger's hope by bringing out their own harmonic treatises and composition tutors using Bach's four-part chorale art as models: J. G. Portmann, *Musikalische Unterricht* (Darmstadt, 1785); Daniel Gottlob Türk, *Von den Wichtigsten Pflichten ein Organist* (Halle, 1787); and Justin Heinrich Knecht, *Gemeinnütziches Elementarwerk der Harmonie und des Generalbasses* (Augsburg, 1792).

43. *Precepts*, 10–11.

44. Schulenberg, 13.

45. Rameau's theory of the fundamental bass has often been misinterpreted by historians as simply pertaining to chordal construction and inversion. (This is unfortunately how Marpurg seems to have read it.) But as I argue in *Rameau and Musical Thought in the Enlightenment* (Cambridge: Cambridge University Press, 1993), the most important and revolutionary component of Rameau's fundamental bass was in its horizontal dimension—its extraordinary ability to model the temporal flow and grammar of chord succession.

himself from Rameau's specter. Still, Rameau's harmonic emphasis was ulti-mately compatible with Kirnberger's outlook, for through it Bach's most ele-vated contrapuntal art could be accounted for within the analytic paradigm of *Reiner Satz.*

Kirnberger inadvertently underscored this point when he argued that "all the things Bach worked out, as complex as some of them may at first appear, can be traced to a fundamental bass composed of natural progressions, and to two simple basic chords: the triad and the essential seventh-chord; and no one will find, in all his doublings, that he ever took any other chord as a basis."[46] The reduction of all harmony to two basic chord types was a central feature of Rameau's theory, and one entirely obscured in Marpurg's writings, whose self-avowed "eclectic" system relied on the independent generation and clas-sification of several dissonant chord types, including all *untergeschobene* chords of the 9th, 11th, and 13th.[47]

We can see a vivid illustration of Kirnberger's application of the funda-mental bass in his analysis of the B-Minor Fugue from Book 1 of the Well-Tempered Clavier. Two sections of this analysis are reproduced in example 2 — in 2a the opening of the fugue, and in 2b a restatement of the fugue subject (in the bass voice towards the end).[48] One can scarcely imagine a more diffi-cult and arguably inappropriate piece to analyze from a Rameauian perspective than the B-Minor Fugue, with its gnarly, twisting subject, dense chromatic writing, and its labyrinthine maze of sharp keys. (The A-Minor Prelude from Well-Tempered Clavier II, which is also analyzed by Kirnberger in this work, is not much more tractable on this account.) Yet it is just for these reasons that Kirnberger must have chosen this monumental piece. Where else could Kirnberger more strikingly display the virtues and insights afforded by his har-

---

46. BR, 449.

47. Marpurg's myopic conception of these chords took Rameau's concept of "supposition" (wherein such chords can be heuristically analyzed as seventh chords with artificial roots "sup-posed" below the bottom) and applied it to all dissonant chords in a completely mechanical and inflexible manner, one that did much to stain Rameau's theory with the reputation of third-stacking.

48. This analysis comes at the end of a small monograph that has often been attributed to J. A. P. Schulz, a student of Kirnberger. (*Die Wahren Grundsätze zum Gebrauch der Harmonie* [Berlin and Königsberg, 1773]). But the analysis itself certainly came from the pen of Kirn-berger, as is testified to by a letter to his publisher (BDOK 3, no. 780).

EX. 2. Johann Kirnberger's "continuo" and fundamental-bass analysis of BWV 869/2 (from Kirnberger, *Die Wahren Grundsätze*, 1773)

monic perspective than in a fugue whose texture is arguably one of the most densely chromatic that Bach ever conceived?

> The following fugue by Johann Sebastian Bach, which to this day has seemed insoluble even to great men of our time, [is here presented] with the basic chords naturally derived from it according to our principles, [and] may serve as evidence for all that we have stated above. We believe that our reasoning is based on the nature of the matter itself, when we assert that these principles of harmony are not only the true ones but also the only ones by which this fugue, as well as all the other apparent difficulties in the works of this greatest harmonist of all times, are solved and made understandable.[49]

Kirnberger is able to subdue the linear chromaticism by first composing in the second system a hypothetical thorough-bass realization of the harmonies he hears underlying the music. Note incidentally how the bass line of this continuo part does not follow strictly the bass voice of the fugue. In Kirnberger's pedagogy, the continuo part forms the essential harmonic skeleton of the music, which is then elaborated thematically by use of diminution. This continuo harmony is itself generated and controlled by the logic of the fundamental bass. In the fifth staff of the analysis, the fundamental bass of the continuo part is revealed, reflecting the use of his so-called incidental dissonances—that is, chords with added ninths and suspensions. In the very bottom system, these dissonances are suppressed, leaving a pure succession of fundamental triads and "essential" seventh chords that proceed almost entirely by falling fifths, with occasional motion by ascending second.

The sufficiency of this analysis suggests why Kirnberger never got around to writing a pedagogy of the fugue, despite his repeated promises to do so.[50] The harmonic pedagogy in his *Kunst* was arguably the sufficient foundation for the fugue—as it was for any kind of composition. Ironically, it was Marpurg—the paragon of a galant critic and self-avowed disciple of Rameau—who wrote the most comprehensive and influential study of the fugue related to

49. BR, 448.

50. The kind of fugal treatise he would write, he often mentioned, would deal not so much with academic problems of fugal entrance and plan, but the rhythmic and metric character of the subject, one based on national dance styles that he believed critical to a successful fugue—and one that set Bach's fugues apart from all others. See his comments in *Gedanken über die verschiedenen Lehrarten in der Komposition, als Vorbereitung zur Fugenkenntniss* (Berlin, 1782).

Bach's practice. But Marpurg's interpretation of the fugue differed profoundly from Kirnberger's, despite his overt acceptance of Rameau's theory. As I have already suggested, it may well have been due to his myopic obsession with Rameau's theory of harmonic generation that he was hindered from interpreting Bach's fugues as harmonic entities in the way Kirnberger did. (Tellingly, there is not a single use of Rameau's fundamental bass in all the pages of Marpurg's *Abhandlung*.)[51] Marpurg drew a greater demarcation between counterpoint and harmony. The concerns of Marpurg in his *Abhandlung* were more geared to the nature of the fugue subject and answer, the kinds of manipulations that may be applied to the subject, and general questions of procedure and form in fugal writings. We can see an illustration of this in his analysis (*Be-(schreibung)*) of the two-part E-Minor Fugue from Book 1 of the Well-Tempered Clavier. Whereas Kirnberger is obviously concerned with the harmonic background to Bach's fugues, Marpurg is concerned with a descriptive taxonomy of each fugal entry, the key in which it occurs, and any transformation by inversion or double counterpoint that may be found.

> The fugue is in e minor and is forty-two measures long in three-four time. The first two measures contain the subject of the exposition. There then follows in measures three and four the answer at whose second beat there appears a countersubject that is very different from the subject. In the fifth measure, the countersubject which first appeared in the upper voice is repeated in the lower one but provided with a new upper part and, by means of a transposition—in fact a clever transposition—together with two additional measures (an even cleverer procedure), it is led into G major. In this key at measure 11 the upper voice thereupon takes up the subject and has the invertible and here inverted countersubject under it. Immediately thereafter the answer appears in the bass in D major as is appropriate to a subject in G major. After this we have a free episode which is also inverted.[52]

51. Indeed, in all his writings, Marpurg never once invokes the fundamental bass as an analytic tool: it was entirely a precompositional heuristic for generating chords. The opposing employments of the fundamental bass by Kirnberger and Marpurg—as analytic and compositional tools, respectively—can be seen as one of the main causes to their later debates over harmonic theory (described in Lester, *Compositional Theory*, 240–56).

52. Quoted in Howard Serwer, "Marpurg versus Kirnberger: Theories of Fugal Composition," *Journal of Music Theory* 14 (1970): 221–22. A related "analysis" of a Bach fugue (the B♭-Minor Fugue from Well-Tempered Clavier II) that resembles this one is to be found in manuscript

The fugue for Marpurg and most of his compatriots was an artful, demanding, and venerable genre. But above all, it was one requiring proper "plan" and
"procedure."

To be sure, Marpurg was concerned with "harmonic" factors, or at least
those that lay within his pseudo-Rameauian paradigm. In their dispute over the
fugue, Marpurg heavily criticized some of Kirnberger's own fugal compositions for inattention to harmonic detail. But the harmonic details that worried
Marpurg were based on a blinkered, chord-by-chord notion of tonality.[53] One
of Marpurg's harshest criticisms of Kirnberger—the improper use of double
counterpoint—was based on his entirely harmonic conception of double counterpoint as representing (and generating) chordal inversions. Kirnberger tried
to rebut Marpurg's criticisms by that tried and true method—citing the practice of Sebastian Bach.[54] But at the time of this dispute (1759), Kirnberger was
still a young composer and theorist, and he had not yet developed his own
thoughts on these questions in any detail. Hence, he was unable to refute effectively any of Marpurg's charges. But with the completion of his *Kunst* some
twenty years later, Kirnberger had in fact worked out a system that could accommodate Marpurg's objections through the synthesis he made of Rameau's
fundamental bass with thorough-bass practice. Indeed, this synthesis allowed
him not only to incorporate Bach's elevated art within the paradigm of four-
part harmony, but also music that was manifestly more galant in style. This
is why Kirnberger would not have seen any inconsistencies between his reverence for Bach's music and his own activities as a composer and pedagogue
of sentimental odes, keyboard dances, and other lightweight genres. (Perhaps
the most striking manifestation of this can be seen in Kirnberger's first and
last publications, each consisting of a short-cut "method" for generating com-

---

(Bds-Mus. Ms. Theor.1023: "Analysis artificiosa Fuga in B molli, mensura 3/2 celeberrimi
authoris J. Sebastiani Bach"). This suggests that however unsophisticated Marpurg's descriptive analysis may be, it was not an uncommon approach in treating the fugue during the
eighteenth century.

53. Hence the dispute cannot be reduced—as Serwer suggests—to Marpurg taking a harmonically "progressive" stance, and Kirnberger a more conservative, contrapuntal view of
the fugue.

54. BDOK 3, no.700.

positions through, respectively, *ars combinatoria* and compositional troping.)[55] Whatever aesthetic distance there may have been between the techniques of strict counterpoint and the kinds of polonaises and sonatas one could concoct with his games, Kirnberger believed all of them to be rooted in pure four-part harmony, even though the overt texture of the music may not reflect this.[56]

There remains, finally, the paradox that Kirnberger adopted almost completely Rameau's fundamental bass while simultaneously assuming the role of Rameau's most energetic critic in Germany. Conversely, Marpurg—who claimed to be promoting this very theory—proved to be an unreliable ambassador. This problem might seem to be only an issue for a historian of music theory. But it is important in the present context since Kirnberger—and subsequent generations of scholars—firmly believed that Rameau's theory was fundamentally incompatible with Bach's compositional practice. A specious but tenacious polarization is thus created, with Rameau and "harmony" on one side and Bach and "counterpoint" on the other, when in reality these components symbiotically interact in Rameau's theory, as they do, of course, in Bach's music.

There seem to be two parts to this story that need to be briefly told. The first concerns the mistransmission of Rameau's theory via Marpurg's translation of d'Alembert's resumé; the second concerns the hostility with which French ideas and culture were received by certain circles of German "patriots" at midcentury. As concerns the first part, let it be noted that Rameau's advocates did not often serve him well. D'Alembert did his best to summarize Rameau's music theory in his widely read redaction, the *Elémens de musique théorique et pratique suivant les principes de M. Rameau* (Paris, 1752), but he failed

---

55. *Der allezeit Fertige Polonoisen und Menuettencomponist* (Berlin, 1757); *Methode, Sonaten aus'm Ermel zu Schüddeln* (Berlin, 1783).

56. Siegfried Borris, *Kirnbergers Leben und Werk und seine Bedeutung im Berliner Musikkreis um 1750* (Kassel: Bärenreiter, 1933), 39ff. That Kirnberger saw no real incompatibility between the various *Schreibarten* and *Gattungen* was made clear in the preface to his lavish edition of Graun's opera ensembles: *Duetti, terzetti, setsetti ed alcuni chori delle opere del Signore Carlo Enrico Graun*, 4 vols. (Berlin, 1773–74). There he pointed out that, despite the overtly galant and Italianate stylisms of this music, it contained some of the most judicious and artful examples of double counterpoint, canon, and other artifices to be found in any literature. "Pure composition" was a necessary component to all good music, no matter what the genre, what the style.

to grasp the more subtle features of that theory. His redaction, for all its clarity, concision, and logic, offered a rather mechanistic and overly deductive picture of Rameau's thought.[57] Unfortunately, this is the picture that was conveyed to German readers when Marpurg undertook to translate d'Alembert's book into German: *Systematische Einleitung in die musicalische Setzkunst, nach den Lehrsätzen des Herrn Rameau* (Leipzig, 1757). This book, combined with Marpurg's own revisions and additions (being a part of his "eclectic" system) ensured that no German reader without access to the French originals would gain an accurate view of the music theory of Herr Rameau.

Thus, when German readers were confronted with the combined "Rameau-Marpurg system," they found an incoherent muddle of acoustical arguments for chord generation, musically insensitive analyses of dissonant suspensions and other nonchord tones, and artificially mechanistic definitions of mode and modulation. It hardly mattered that this "system" perverted Rameau's own views; for many German musicians of the time, it was enough that it was a theory with Rameau's name on it. And because there was a strong prejudice against matters French among many Berlin musicians who chafed under the suffocating domination of French culture (if not repertoire) at Frederick's court, "Rameau's" theory may have been received as one more cultural insult.

We can now understand that when Kirnberger and Marpurg became embroiled once again in the 1770s, this time debating issues related to tuning and Rameau's theory, Bach's name was once again drawn into the fray as much for political reasons as for genuine artistic ones. If for the cosmopolitan Marpurg there was little problem in reconciling his enthusiasm for Rameau with his proclaimed admiration for Bach, for the more provincial Kirnberger no reconciliation was possible. Believing Bach's compositions to represent the greatest repertoire of true, indigenous German music, Kirnberger (and Carl Philipp Emanuel) simply could not tolerate some French author or his surrogate presuming to explain the theoretical basis of this music.[58] Marpurg tried vainly to

57. It would far exceed the boundaries of the present essay to discuss here the full nature of these differences, or to analyze the causes for the opposing epistemologies of Rameau and d'Alembert. Such a discussion can be found, though, in my *Rameau and Musical Thought in the Enlightenment*, 252–90.

58. Sensitive to just this charge, Reichardt felt the need to plead Rameau's case when he introduced an issue of his music magazine with an article on French music. Rameau's harmonic

keep Bach out of the debate, perhaps sensing that he would have trouble competing with Kirnberger's authority when it came to matters of Bach's compositional pedagogy:

> Great Heavens! Why must old Bach be drawn by main force into a dispute in which, if he were still alive, he certainly would have taken no part. I believe that this great man made use of more than one single method in his teaching, fitting the method to the capacities of each head with which he had to deal, according to whether he found it equipped with greater or smaller natural gifts, stiffer or more flexible, wooden or full of spirit. But I am also assured that if there exist anywhere any manuscript introductions to harmony by this man, certain things will be sought in vain among them which Mr. Kirnberger wants to sell us as Bach's teaching principles. His famous son in Hamburg ought to know something about this, too.[59]

This was obviously a strategic error by Marpurg, for Carl Philipp Emanuel had not too much earlier completed a similar polemic with Christoph Nichelmann—his former colleague and harpsichord rival in Berlin—in which Rameau's theory also had played a central role. While the arguments between Nichelmann and Carl Philipp Emanuel were not as overtly theoretical as were those between Kirnberger and Marpurg, they did engage the two issues relevant here: the value of Rameau's fundamental bass as an analytic explanation (this time as interpreted by Nichelmann), and the authority to speak about J. S. Bach's music. Reacting partly to the kind of analysis illustrated in example 1, but more strongly to Nichelmann's undiplomatic penchant to criticize and rewrite the music of others (including compositions by both C. P. E. and his father), C. P. E. issued a strongly worded pamphlet attacking Nichelmann's treatise.[60] While it would take us far afield here to discuss the specific

theory could be reconciled with Bach's music, Reichardt argued, as it was based on universal tonal principles that Bach understood instinctively (BDOK 3, no. 863).

59. BR, 449–50.

60. Issued under the pseudonym of Caspar Dünkelfeind: *Gedanken eines Liebhabers der Tonkunst über Herrn Nichelmanns Tractat von der Melodie* (Berlin, 1755). While the authorship of C. P. E. cannot be proven definitively, I have elsewhere argued that internal evidence strongly points to him as the author: "Nichelmann Contra C. Ph. E. Bach: Harmonic Theory and Musical Politics at the Court of Frederick the Great," in *Carl Philipp Emanuel Bach und die*

issues of the polemic, suffice it to say that political reasons were equally at play. Nichelmann's close association with Rameau's theory must have exacerbated in C. P. E.'s mind the polarity between the Frenchman and J. S. Bach. Thus, when Kirnberger called upon C. P. E. to respond to Marpurg's challenge, the results were predictable: "Moreover, what Mr. Bach, Capellmeister in Hamburg, thinks of the excellent work of Mr. Marpurg, is shown by some passages from a letter that this famous man has written me: 'The behavior of Mr. Marpurg towards you is execrable.' Further: 'That my basic principles and those of my late father are anti-Rameau you may loudly proclaim.'" [61]

But there is nothing in Rameau's theory that is intrinsically and irredeemably opposed to Bach's music, as Kirnberger's own analyses powerfully demonstrate. It was Marpurg's perversion of that theory against which C. P. E. and Kirnberger were really fighting. But by this point, the real origins of the various positions held by each combatant had become hopelessly obscured.

\* \* \*

It is tempting for us today to speculate what Bach would have said in response to the arguments of his quarrelsome disciples. Where would the statue have stood? Bach's apparent silence on questions of music theory did not mean he lacked distinct points of view, nor the spleen to express them when he felt it important to do so. We need only recall the pugnacity and stubbornness with which he carried on his arguments with Ernesti, or for that matter, the obvious covert support he gave to writers like Birnbaum and Schröter when they wrote on his behalf.

Lacking any secure documentary evidence, a natural place for us to look is the music itself. If we recall that *theoria* in its most fundamental sense means to "contemplate" fully and completely, then Bach's approach to composition is arguably "theoretical." Since Forkel, observers have noted how Bach takes some thematic or harmonic idea in his compositions and systematically develops it—whether it be through fugal invention, canonic art, or diminution. This is why many nineteenth-century theorists dubbed his late instrumental

---

*europäische Musikkultur des mittleren 18. Jahrhunderts*, ed. Hans-Joachim Marx (Göttingen: Vandenhoeck & Ruprecht, 1990), 189–220.

61. BR, 450.

cycles like the Goldberg Variations and the Art of Fugue "learned," "speculative," and finally, "theoretical."[62] From a historical perspective, they represent a kind of encyclopedic summa in the tradition of seventeenth-century scholastic inquiry; they constitute an implicit Mattheis of technique and potential that bespeaks far more than any overtly didactic treatise could of the author's grasp of music's material, formal, and efficient causes (to express this in the Aristotelian terminology that would have been familiar to so many music theorists of Bach's day). Perhaps, then, Bach was a theorist after all. But to paraphrase Leibniz, if music is the counting of numbers by the mind unaware it is doing so, we can say that Bach was a composer who was theorizing yet unaware of doing so.

Of course, this still does not tell us Bach's view on the more mundane (or perhaps, rarified) theoretical issues that so vexed and divided his followers. Like the scriptures of Luther's Bible, Bach's compositions were not open to easy exegesis. Bach's music invites conflicting interpretations, being a quodlibet of different styles and functions, and all theorists who cite his music in their arguments—in the eighteenth century as well as today—can find justification somewhere. However, rather than agonize over a resolution to this question, though, perhaps we can find consolation in Jaroslav Pelikan's wise monograph published a decade ago—and whose title I have borrowed for the present study.[63] As to the question whether Bach's theological convictions were orthodox or Pietist, or for that matter, his world view that of the *Aufklärung* or the Reformation, Pelikan concluded that no fixed answer was possible, since Bach seemed to offer evidence suggestive to all sides. But maybe it is the question that is wrong, Pelikan averred. Perhaps we have set up a polarity between two irreconcilable extremes, when in fact there is only a continuum. If Bach's position among the theologians is Delphic, so it is with his place among the theorists. His music constitutes a spectrum—really a whole musical ocean, to paraphrase Beethoven—that is large enough to accommodate all the harmonic theories, theological catechisms, and numerological encodings his lis-

---

62. For an enlightening discussion of nineteenth-century reactions to Bach's fugal art, as well as a selected anthology of analytic excerpts, see Ian Bent, *Music Analysis in the Nineteenth Century*, vol. 1 (Cambridge: Cambridge University Press, 1994), esp. 21–28.

63. Jaroslav Pelikan, *Bach among the Theologians* (Philadelphia: Fortress, 1986).

teners have found in it over the ages. It is also large enough to accommodate our concerns today, our own peculiar postmodern urges to project upon it differing hermeneutic readings, political allegories, and social or gender hierarchies. That is perhaps Bach's most tenacious theoretical legacy, and one that promises not to exhaust itself any time soon.

# Bach and Mozart's Artistic Maturity

### Robert L. Marshall

In the annals of musicological writing, few questions have been rehearsed so often, or for so long, as that of Mozart's relationship to Bach and the significance of that relationship for subsequent music history. The traditional, and still predominant, understanding of Mozart's relationship with Bach, reduced to its essentials, runs as follows. About a year after he had settled in Vienna, and by early 1782 at the latest, Mozart came to know the music of J. S. Bach during the course of his weekly Sunday musical matinees at the home of Baron Gottfried van Swieten. This exposure and confrontation, this *Auseinandersetzung* with the music of Bach profoundly and permanently influenced, indeed virtually transformed, Mozart's style and even reshaped his fundamental understanding of the nature and potential of music. The result was a major aesthetic and stylistic breakthrough—one that effected a synthesis of the "learned" and the "galant," of Bachian counterpoint and complexity and rococo "naturalness" and immediacy. The result was nothing less than the creation of the Viennese Classical Style.

This familiar argument, a virtual truism not only of Mozart biography but of music history and still by far the prevailing view, has in fact been challenged—and by some distinguished authorities. Sides have been taken. Since the question has become controversial, a brief review of the history of the historiography is in order. The first attempt to assess the larger historical importance of Mozart's Bach reception—as opposed simply to noting that Mozart knew and admired Bach's music—was offered by one of Mozart's own acquaintances, the Abbé Maximilian Stadler (1748-1843). In his *Materialien zu einer Geschichte der Musik*, compiled between 1815 and 1829, Stadler remarks: "Owing especially to those works of his written during the last ten years in Vienna, Mozart propelled himself to such heights that he was acknowledged, not only in Vienna but throughout Germany, indeed throughout all of Europe, as the greatest master, *one who united within himself Sebastian Bach's art, Handel's strength, Haydn's most witty clarity and charm*" (emphasis added).[1] Since then, all has been Variations on the Theme. For example, Constanze Mozart's second husband, Georg Nikolaus Nissen, clearly appropriating Stadler's insight, wrote the following in the *Anhang* to the first full-length biography of Mozart (published in 1828):

> After [composers], with the exception of but a few masters, and in the interest of achieving a light, popular, sentimental style had distanced themselves ever more from the thoroughness of old Sebastian Bach, Mozart appeared, who, filled with deep admiration for Bach, combined in his own compositions Italian charm, German strength, and most notably Bachian art (specifically with respect to richness of harmony, melodically informed bass lines, and contrapuntal treatment, altogether); and along with Joseph Haydn he founded a new epoch in the art of music, the one with which the modern style began.[2]

In this century, Hermann Abert devoted an entire chapter of his monumental Mozart biography to demonstrating the same proposition. The chapter is entitled "Die große Stilwandlung unter dem Einfluß Seb. Bachs, Händels und Ph. E. Bachs."[3] The thesis attained its classic—or perhaps one should say, its Romantic—formulation in Alfred Einstein's *Mozart: His Character, His Work*, in a chapter entitled "Mozart and Counterpoint." Einstein writes: "For Mozart the encounter with [Bach's] compositions resulted in a revolution and a crisis

1. "Durch diese seine besonders die letzteren zehn Jahre in Wien geschriebenen Kunstwerke schwang sich Mozart so in die Höhe, daß er sowohl in Wienn als ganz Deutschland, in ganz Europa als der größte Meister anerkannt wurde, welcher Sebastian Bachs Kunst, Händels Stärke, Haydns launigste Klarheit und Anmuth in sich verband." Quoted in Martin Zenck, *Die Bach-Rezeption des späten Beethoven* (Stuttgart: Franz Steiner, 1986), 83.

2. Nissen, *Anhang zu W. A. Mozarts Biographie* (Leipzig, 1828; reprint, Hildesheim: Georg Olms, 1972), 25–26: "Nachdem man allmählig mehr auf das Leichte, Populäre, Sentimentale hinarbeitend, mit Ausnahme weniger Meister, sich immer weiter von der alten Seb. Bach'schen Gründlichkeit entfernt hatte, trat Mozart auf, der, mit tiefer Verehrung für Bach erfüllt, in seinen eigenen Compositionen, italienische Anmuth mit deutscher Kraft, und merklich mit Bach'scher Kunst (in Reichthume der Harmonie und in den melodischen figurirten Bässen, in contrapunctischer Behandlung überhaupt) verknüpfte, und nebst Jos. Haydn eine neue Epoche der Tonkunst begründete, mit welcher derjenige moderne Styl begann."

3. Hermann Abert, *W. A. Mozart: Neubearbeitete und erweiterte Ausgabe von Otto Jahns Mozart* (Leipzig, 1923; reprint, Leipzig: VEB Breitkopf & Härtel, 1956).

in his creative activity." He continues: "Mozart was never completely finished with this experience, but it enriched his imagination and resulted in more and more perfect works."[4]

In recent years the theme has been echoed and developed further by, among others, Charles Rosen, Ludwig Finscher, and Robert Marshall. Early in *The Classical Style*, Charles Rosen observes: "In spite of Mozart's acquaintance with later composers who tried to continue the contrapuntal tradition, a remarkable development comes over his work from the moment he begins to know the music of Johann Sebastian Bach."[5]

According to Ludwig Finscher,

> Mozart's decisive breakthrough to the classical style, his contribution to the elaboration of this style as a synthesis which one can, with some justification, describe as a Universal style, one in which the historically older idea of a synthesis of national styles was lifted, this breakthrough took place not in the symphony, indeed not really in any particular genre, but primarily in the context of a biographical situation, in which Mozart's lifelong practice of coming to terms with various stylistic models culminated in the confrontation, practically simultaneously, with two artistically overwhelming impressions: the encounter with Bach and Handel in the house of Baron van Swieten and the encounter with Haydn's String Quartets, Opus 33.[6]

Elsewhere Finscher puts it more cogently: "The year 1782 [thanks to the encounter with Bach, Handel, and Haydn's op. 33 string quartets] thus becomes

4. Alfred Einstein, *Mozart: His Character, His Work*, trans. Arthur Mendel and Nathan Broder (New York: Oxford University Press, 1945), 151, 153.

5. Charles Rosen, *The Classical Style: Haydn, Mozart, Beethoven* (New York: W. W. Norton & Co., 1972), 20 n.1.

6. Ludwig Finscher, "Mozart und die Idee eines musikalischen Universalstils," in *Neues Handbuch der Musikwissenschaft 5: Die Musik des 18. Jahrhunderts*, ed. Carl Dahlhaus (Laaber: Laaber-Verlag, 1985), 274: "Der entscheidende Durchbruch Mozarts zum klassischen Stil, sein Beitrag zur Ausbildung dieses Stils als einer Synthese, die man mit einigem Recht als Universalstil bezeichnen kann und in der die historisch ältere Idee einer Synthese der Nationalstile aufgehoben wurde, gelang nicht in der Symphonie, überhaupt nicht eigentlich in einer Gattung, sondern primär durch eine biographische Situation, in der sich die lebenslang eingeübte Auseinandersetzung mit Mustern zur praktisch gleichzeitigen Konfrontation mit zwei künstlerisch überwältigenden Eindrücken zuspitzte: der Begegnung mit Bach und Händel im Hause des Barons van Swieten und der Begegnung mit Haydns Streichquartetten opus 33."

an epochal year, indeed the year in which the classical style was born—and presiding over the birth are Bach and Handel."[7]

As for Marshall, a 1991 essay, "Bach and Mozart: Styles of Musical Genius," opens with this form of the conventional wisdom: "It is well known that Mozart was profoundly impressed by, and influenced by, the music of Johann Sebastian Bach. Indeed, his mature style is unimaginable without it."[8]

This view, although it is the prevailing opinion, is not unanimous. Several eminent Mozarteans have questioned the ultimate importance of Mozart's Bach experience. The challenge was apparently first issued by Stanley Sadie in a brief article, "Mozart, Bach and Counterpoint."[9] Sadie asks: "Did Mozart's contact with Bach, as Einstein claimed, really cause a 'revolution and a crisis in his creative activity'?" After considering the well-known fugal examples, Sadie concludes that "Mozart undoubtedly had the utmost reverence for Bach as a supreme master of his craft; but I fancy he would have been amused, or perhaps mildly offended, at the notion of anyone so absurdly out of date affecting his music in anything more than the most superficial ways."[10]

There is at least a trace of debunking skepticism, too, in Neal Zaslaw's comment, early in his magisterial study of Mozart's symphonies: "Much has been made of Wolfgang's encounter in the early 1780s with J. S. Bach's contrapuntal style, but sufficient recognition has not always been given to the fact that Wolfgang grew up surrounded by composers who prided themselves on their command of the *stile antico*."[11] This comment, by the way, is in effect the only substantial reference at all to J. S. Bach in Zaslaw's massive volume. Finally, Ulrich Konrad, in his recent comprehensive investigation of

7. Ludwig Finscher, "Bach—Mozart," in *Sommerakademie Johann Sebastian Bach: Almanach* (Stuttgart, 1982), v/18–29: "Das Jahr 1782 wird so zum Epochenjahr, zum eigentlichen Geburtsjahr des klassischen Stils, und die Geburtshelfer sind Bach und Händel." Finscher's original German is obviously both more cogent and more eloquent, thanks mainly to the untranslatable "Geburtshelfer"—unless one is prepared to accept "midwives" with reference to Bach and Handel.

8. Robert L. Marshall, "Bach and Mozart: Styles of Musical Genius," *Bach: Journal of the Riemenschneider Bach Institute* 22, no.1 (1991): 16–32, at p.16.

9. Stanley Sadie, "Mozart, Bach and Counterpoint," *Musical Times* 105 (1964): 23–24.

10. Ibid., 24.

11. Neal Zaslaw, *Mozart's Symphonies: Context, Performance Practice, Reception* (Oxford: Clarendon Press, 1989), 9–10.

the Mozart sketches, cites and essentially endorses Sadie's position: "Let the opinion at the least be voiced that the constant emphasis on both Constanze Mozart's alleged passion for fugues, which is supposed to have stimulated her husband, as well as the encounter of the composer with the music of Johann Sebastian Bach—which, especially in the German-language literature has virtually taken on the aura of a mythos—that these observations do not essentially advance the goal of an objective assessment of the historical and, above all, the musical implications of Mozart's contrapuntal thought."[12]

Despite such recent doubts, however, the familiar, traditional understanding, at least in this writer's opinion, still retains its validity. However, as the reservations that have been raised concerning the "mythos" (in Konrad's characterization) make clear, a number of qualifications are called for.

In the first place, it is, at best, misleading to draw a close parallel between Mozart's confrontation with the music of Bach and Handel, and J. S. Bach's encounter with sixteenth-century polyphony. When Bach embarked on his serious investigation of the *stile antico* in the mid-1730s, Palestrina had been dead for close to 150 years; when Mozart began his extensive study of J. S. Bach, Bach had been dead for just over thirty. The relation between Bach and Mozart, in short, is not at all analogous to that between Bach and Palestrina. Bach belonged to the generation of Mozart's grandparents and was the father of one of Mozart's mentors, Johann Christian Bach. By the same token, Bach's music, for Mozart, was not representative of a historical style (not yet) nor part of a historicizing movement—as it was to be for Beethoven. Bach's music represented a *stile antico* for Mozart no more, perhaps, than the music of Bartók or Stravinsky represents a *stile antico* for us.

\* \* \*

Johann Sebastian Bach's name appears in the Mozart family correspondence for the first time in Wolfgang's famous letter to Nannerl from Vienna, dated

12. Ulrich Konrad, *Mozarts Schaffensweise* (Göttingen: Vandenhoeck & Ruprecht, 1992), 470: "Wenigstens die Meinung sei geäußert daß die ständige Betonung sowohl von Constanze Mozarts angeblicher Fugenleidenschaft, die den Gatten stimuliert habe, als auch von der besonders im deutschsprachigen Schrifttum beinahe zum Mythos stilisierten Begnung des Komponisten mit der Musik Johann Sebastian Bachs die sachliche Beurteilung der historischen und vor allem musikalischen Implikationen von Mozarts kontrapunktischem Denken nicht wesentlich fördern. . . . (Vernünftigerweise sollte man fragen, mit welcher Lernabsicht genau Mozart Fugen von Bach und Händel nachschreiben wollte)."

10 April 1782: "I go every Sunday at 12 o'clock to the Baron van Swieten, where nothing is played but Handel and Bach. I am collecting at the moment the fugues of Bach—not only of Sebastian but also of Emanuel and Friedemann."[13]

It is hard not to get the impression from the standard biographical literature that these Sunday matinees at the Baron van Swieten's marked the beginning of Mozart's serious encounter with the music of Bach. But it seems clear from the way Mozart introduces the names of Bach—father and sons—that they were not unfamiliar to Nannerl and needed no particular identification or further description. Indeed, Mozart's knowledge of Bach's music most likely antedated the Van Swieten sessions by decades.

The constellation of evidence for this contention begins, not surprisingly, with Leopold Mozart. In the early 1750s, Leopold Mozart had connections with at least one important member of the Berlin Bach circle: Friedrich Wilhelm Marpurg (1718–95). Marpurg's connections with Bach are well known. Most notably, he was the author of the preface to the second edition of the Art of Fugue (published in 1752), and in his *Abhandlung von der Fuge* (1753/54) he drew extensively on the music of J. S. Bach for his examples. As for Leopold Mozart's connections with Marpurg, in 1756 Marpurg had published a favorable review of Leopold's violin treatise in his *Historisch-Kritische Beyträge zur Aufnahme der Musik*; in the following year, and in the same journal, he printed Leopold's "Report on the Present State of the Musical Establishment at the Court of His Serene Highness the Archbishop of Salzburg in the Year 1757." It seems safe to assume that Marpurg had commissioned the contribution from Leopold a year or so earlier.[14]

Whether or not Leopold's connections with Marpurg involved the music of J. S. Bach is not known. But it is certainly a good possibility. Be that as it may, it is more than likely that Leopold had become aware of Bach's music considerably earlier than the 1750s, namely, as a student in his native Augsburg. During

---

13. *The Letters of Mozart and His Family*, ed. Emily Anderson, 3d ed. (London: Macmillan, 1985), 800. *Mozart Briefe und Aufzeichnungen: Gesamtausgabe*, ed. Wilhelm A. Bauer and Otto Erich Deutsch (Kassel: Bärenreiter, 1963) 3:201: "[I]ch gehe alle Sonntage um 12 uhr zum Baron von Suiten—und da wird nichts gespiellt als Händl und Bach.—ich mach mir eben eine Collection von den Bachischen fugen.—so wohl sebastian als Emanuel und friedeman Bach."

14. "Nachricht von dem gegenwärtigen Zustande der Musik Sr. Hochfürstl. Gnaden des Erzbischoffs zu Salzburg im Jahr 1757" (Zaslaw, *Mozart's Symphonies*, 2, n.1). A complete English translation of Leopold's "Report" appears in Zaslaw's volume as Appendix C.

Leopold's youth, the cantor of the Protestant church in Augsburg, St. Anne's, was Philipp David Kräuter (1690–1741). Kräuter, a native of Augsburg, had been a pupil of Johann Sebastian Bach's in Weimar in 1712 and 1713.[15] As several scholars have suggested, Leopold "doubtless" heard performances by Kräuter in Augsburg in his youth and they "probably" included music by J. S. Bach.[16]

Finally, in addition to Marpurg in Berlin and Kräuter in Augsburg, Leopold had also had some contact with one of Bach's leading champions in Leipzig: Lorenz Christoph Mizler (1711–78). As is well known, Mizler, in the year 1747, inducted J. S. Bach (whom he described as his "good friend and patron") into his *Korrespondierende Sozietät der Musicalischen Wissenschaften* as its fourteenth member. Considerably less well known is the fact that in 1753 Mizler had extended an invitation of membership into his prestigious society to Leopold Mozart. (Whether Leopold ever accepted the invitation is not clear.)[17]

As for Wolfgang, it seems reasonable to assume, in light of Leopold's likely acquaintance with J. S. Bach's music, that he had exposed Wolfgang to it as a young child. And if not Leopold in Salzburg, then surely Johann Christian Bach in London. Indeed, our suspicions concerning an early Wolfgang Mozart–Sebastian Bach connection rise above the level of circumstantial evidence and assume something resembling documented verification in the following passage from Franz Niemetschek's 1798 *Life of Mozart*. Referring to the Mozarts' grand tour to Paris and London in 1764 and 1765, Niemetschek reports: "In Paris and London, pieces by Handel and Bach were placed before him [Wolfgang], which to the astonishment of all experts he was immediately able to perform with accuracy and with proper expression."[18] We may be reasonably sure that by the late 1790s the "Bach" Niemetschek had in mind with his conjunction of the names of Handel and Bach was Johann Sebastian.

Finally, evidence of a more tangible, and audible, sort is provided by a

15. BDOK 2, no. 58.

16. Reinhold Hammerstein, "Der Gesang der geharnischten Männer: Eine Studie zu Mozarts Bachbild," *Archiv für Musikwissenschaft* 13 (1956): 1–24, at p. 13; also Ernst Fritz Schmid, *Ein schwäbisches Mozartbuch* (Stuttgart: Alfons-Bürger, 1948), 90.

17. See Abert, *W. A. Mozart* 1:5; also the article on Mizler by George J. Buelow, in *The New Grove Dictionary of Music and Musicians*, ed. Stanley Sadie (London: Macmillan, 1980), 12: 372–73.

18. Franz Niemetschek, *Life of Mozart*, trans. Helen Mautner (London: Leonard Hyman, 1956), 21.

EX. 1. Mozart, Fugue in G Minor, K. 401, opening

EX. 2. *a*, BWV 867/2, subject.
*b*, BWV 1080/1, subject

musical composition: Mozart's fragmentary (i.e., almost finished) Fugue in G Minor for "Clavier," K. 401/375e.[19] Whether this piece is for organ or piano or harpsichord, for two hands or four hands, has been a matter of dispute. What has never been in dispute is the manifest Bachian influence to be seen and heard in it (ex. 1).

It is hard to imagine how Mozart could have composed, or even have imagined composing, such an atypical piece—moreover, a contrapuntal tour de force of the first order: a counter-double fugue, that is, a double fugue whose two subjects are inversions of one another—if he had remained in sublime ignorance of the Art of Fugue or the Well-Tempered Clavier. The idea is even more inconceivable, given the frequently observed and, indeed, impossible-to-overlook similarities between Mozart's subject and those of both the B♭-minor fugue from Book 1 of the Well-Tempered Clavier and the Art of Fugue (ex. 2).

The connection is especially strong with the Art of Fugue, since, in addition to the family resemblance of the subjects, the same compositional techniques are explored. Indeed, it seems to have been Mozart's objective to "trump" his model, insofar as his fugue unites within a single composition the "agendas" of no fewer than three of Bach's pieces from the Art of Fugue: two of the simple fugues based, respectively, on the *rectus* and *inversus* forms of the subject, along with the Contrapunctus No. 5 (in the numbering of the original edition) in

19. Only the last 8 bars of the 103-measure composition are not by Mozart. The work was completed by Abbé Stadler.

which both forms are combined (see ex. 3).[20] So "Bachian" is this fugue, and so impressive, if admittedly rather dry and "academic" in its technical mastery, that it has been confidently dated by all commentators (until fairly recently) to Mozart's Vienna period and specifically to Mozart's "Bach year," 1782. It is now known, however, that the work was composed a full decade earlier than that. Wolfgang Plath demonstrated some twenty years ago, on the basis of the handwriting in the autograph, that the composition was in all likelihood composed a full ten years earlier than has been universally assumed, namely, in the late summer of 1772.[21]

Mozart scholarship, it seems, has not yet fully come to terms with the implications of this discovery, the most significant of which, clearly, is that Mozart not only knew, but had already begun his *Auseinandersetzung* with J. S. Bach's most significant and challenging contrapuntal keyboard music by the early 1770s. This, of course, again raises the question as to the source of this exposure. If it was not the good Baron van Swieten, then who? Evidence already presented above strongly suggests both Leopold and J. C. Bach as plausible intermediaries. But an even more likely candidate is worth consideration.

It is known that Padre Martini, who among other things was the teacher of Johann Christian Bach in the late 1750s and an admirer of Johann Sebastian Bach during the composer's lifetime, owned a fragmentary but musically complete copy of a print of the Musical Offering as early as April 1750. He also possessed a manuscript copy of much of the E-minor Partita, from *Clavierübung* I,[22] and most likely *Clavierübung* III as well. (At all events he quotes the opening of *Dies sind die heilgen zehn Gebot*, BWV 678, in his *Storia della Musica*.)[23] Therefore, it would have been altogether consistent with his interests as a contrapuntist (and with his passion as a bibliophile) for him also to have

20. See Hans Dennerlein, *Der unbekannte Mozart: Die Welt seiner Klavierwerke* (Leipzig: Breitkopf & Härtel, 1951), 165–67.

21. Wolfgang Plath, "Beiträge zur Mozart-Autographie II: Schriftchronologie 1770–1780," *Mozart-Jahrbuch 1976/77*, 161. The watermark studies of Alan Tyson corroborate a pre-Viennese dating of the paper of this autograph. See *Neue Mozart-Ausgabe* X/33/2: *Supplement: Wasserzeichen-Katalog* (Kassel: Bärenreiter, 1992), *Textband*, 52: "Wasserzeichen II."

22. See BDOK 2, nos. 597a, 600.

23. See BDOK 3, no. 689.

acquired a copy of the Art of Fugue—through J. C. Bach or others—well before the visit of the Mozarts to Bologna in 1770.

It is important to keep in mind that Mozart's involvement with the fugue in the early and mid-1770s, while, on the one hand, remarkable and perhaps unique with respect to its specific evocation of J. S. Bach and in its breathtaking display of the most sophisticated contrapuntal virtuosity, was, on the other hand, symptomatic of the newly kindled infatuation with traditional fugal procedures among Austrian composers at the time. Hitherto largely a specialized stylistic device, mainly identified with music for the church and ritualistically associated with a few traditional moments in the mass and elsewhere, the new phenomenon, as is well known, now introduced contrapuntal and fugal procedures into secular instrumental ensemble music as well. It also had aesthetic and ideological connections with the so-called Sturm und Drang episode of the mid-1770s. Its full dimensions, at least for the chamber music of the period, have been copiously documented by Warren Kirkendale.[24]

Among the best-known manifestations of this trendy contrapuntal fashion are the "learned," and not a little pretentious, fugal finales in three of Haydn's op. 20 string quartets (composed 1771) and, in emulation of them, Mozart's String Quartets in F Major and D Minor, K.168 and K.173 respectively, composed in late summer 1773. These compositions, however, for all their fugal expositions, stretti, inversions, and retrogrades, have essentially little, if anything, to do with J. S. Bach. They reflect, rather, textbook models and are more than a little dependent on stereotypical thematic and contrapuntal formulas, such as the descending chromatic soggetto of Mozart's K.173 or the venerable falling fifth, falling diminished seventh, subject of Haydn's F-minor quartet finale (ex. 4). (The latter archetype is clearly discernible as well, to a greater or lesser degree, in the subjects of Bach's Musical Offering, Art of Fugue, and Mozart's K.401.)

However, one important literary source, technically and *ideologically*, for this renewed interest in the venerable, if nearly moribund (but not yet quite extinct), strict, or learned, style in composition does exhibit specific connections to J. S. Bach: the writings of the Berlin theorists Marpurg and, especially,

24. Warren Kirkendale, *Fuge und Fugato in der Kammermusik des Rokoko und der Klassik* (Tutzing: Hans Schneider, 1966).

EX. 3. *a*, BWV 1080, Opening of Contrapunctus 1, 3, and 5.
*b*, K. 401, mm. 1–3, 46–48, 81–84

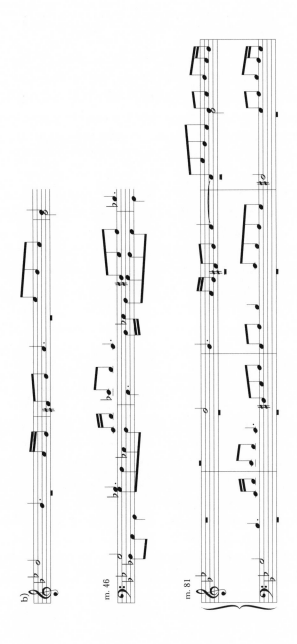

EX. 4. Haydn, String Quartet, op. 20/5, finale, opening theme

Johann Philipp Kirnberger, whose advocacy of the *Kunst des Reinen Satzes* caught fire during the 1770s in Vienna. There was, then, in this respect, a transmission to Mozart, along with other Austrian composers, of what we may describe as a specifically Bachian ethos, regarding "serious" or "strict" composition.

Most important and obvious is the fact that the more imaginative composers of the time recognized the aesthetic potential of transforming a textbook thematic stereotype—such as the tonic-to-dominant-plus-diminished-seventh leap, for example—if one were to remove it from the domain of the merely pedagogical and aim to release its inherently powerful expressive properties. Doing so could introduce into the sphere of the hitherto innocuous symphony, for example, in place of the routine major-mode arpeggio fanfares in the opening allegros that passed for "themes," a more serious, more intense, more personal thematic statement. An example that comes readily to mind is the opening of Mozart's Symphony in G Minor, K.183/173dB, composed by 5 October 1773 (ex. 5).

We owe, then, to this retrospective return to late Baroque melodic convention the invention of something quite new in symphonic writing: what we may call the "Passionate Allegro Theme." There was also the recognition of the dramatic, even heroic, potential, of such an academic contrapuntal device as stretto, if strategically introduced (perhaps in the course of a development section). An example can be found in the same movement (ex. 6).

Broadly speaking, these symptoms of the Sturm und Drang phenomenon are perhaps best understood as part of a general reaction against (even disgust with) the facile, galant/rococo, minimalist aesthetic that had permeated and dominated European musical culture for some fifty years, since the 1720s. It is easy to see how this style would not wear well in the long run, and could not satisfy any truly formidably equipped composer—a Haydn or a Mozart. By the 1770s, the complex, intellectually challenging, deeply expressive music of Bach was literally waiting to be (re)discovered. Its (re)discovery was perhaps as inevitable as anything in history, or at least in art history, can ever be:

EX. 5. Mozart: Symphony in G Minor, K.183/1 opening theme

the most gifted composers of the 1770s and 1780s were underchallenged and undernourished, and they were thirsting for such nourishment and challenge as the music of Johann Sebastian Bach could provide. This was true, too, of course, not only for composers, but also for the most thoughtful connoisseurs: a Baron van Swieten, for example.

\* \* \*

All of the foregoing notwithstanding, I do not wish to disavow the conventional wisdom proclaiming the signal importance of the year 1782 and of the weekly performances at the home of Baron van Swieten. The conventional wisdom is correct: the significance of those sessions cannot be overestimated; they were of decisive importance for Mozart's later artistic development. But our understanding of the precise nature of their significance, and of the ways in which Mozart henceforth approached and appropriated the music of Bach needs to be, if not altogether reevaluated, nonetheless modified.

The year 1782 does indeed represent the period, if not of Mozart's first encounter, then of his first extended, intensive, and systematic study of the keyboard music of J. S. Bach, along with the oratorios of Handel. Mozart wrote to his sister on 20 April 1782 that "The Baron van Swieten . . . gave me all the works of Handel and Sebastian Bach to take home with me (after I had played them to him)."[25]

Van Swieten had served as Habsburg "ambassador extraordinary" at the Prussian court from 1770 to 1777. While in Berlin he belonged to the circle of Princess Anna Amalia. Like the Princess he was a pupil of Kirnberger's, through whom—and also through none other than Frederick the Great himself—van Swieten became a fervent admirer of the music of J. S. Bach. He

25. *The Letters of Mozart and His Family*, 801.

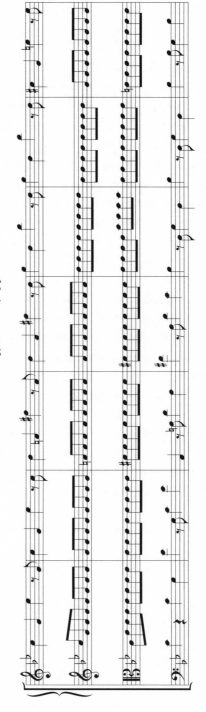

EX. 6. K.183/1, mm. 87–93

later became close to C. P. E. Bach in Hamburg. We know that the works in the Baron's possession included the Two- and Three-Part Inventions, the French and English Suites, the Partitas, a copy containing the fugues of the Well-Tempered Clavier, the Musical Offering, Part III of the *Clavierübung*, the six organ sonatas, BWV 525–30, arranged for two claviers—even a copy of the Magnificat that had been prepared from the original autograph, which had been in C. P. E. Bach's possession.[26]

Mozart's confrontation with the music of J. S. Bach under the aegis of Van Swieten passed through at least three—possibly four—distinct phases that may be characterized as transcription, imitation, assimilation and synthesis, and transcendence.

*Stage 1:* Conscientious, indeed reverential, transcription. This consisted of making arrangements of Bach's fugues, taken mainly from the Well-Tempered Clavier (but from other sources as well), for strings: quartet and probably trio (perhaps also string quintet). K. 405, which survives in Mozart's autograph, consists of five four-part fugues from Book 2 of the Well-Tempered Clavier, arranged for string quartet.[27] Another series, K. 404a (whose authenticity has been challenged but is largely accepted), consists of six three-part fugues arranged for string trio. This time they are all provided with newly composed preludes, most of them presumably by Mozart.[28]

26. On van Swieten's career see the article by Edward Olleson in *The New Grove Dictionary*, 18:414-15. On van Swieten's library, see Andreas Holschneider, "Die musikalische Bibliothek Gottfried van Swietens," in *Bericht über den internationalen musikwissenschaftlichen Kongress Kassel 1962* (Kassel: Bärenreiter, 1963), 174-78.

27. They are the first five four-part fugues from the set: namely, those in C minor, D major, D♯ minor (here in D minor), E-flat major, and E major.

28. Three are from the Well-Tempered Clavier. From Book 1: no. 8 in D♯ minor (here in D minor); from Book 2: nos. 14 in F♯ minor (here in G minor) and 13 in F♯ major (here in F major). The group also contains Contrapunctus 8 from the Art of Fugue, preceded by the F-major Adagio from the D-minor Organ Trio, BWV 527, which serves as a prelude to the Contrapunctus; also movements 2 and 3 from the C-minor Organ Trio, BWV 526, presented here as a prelude and fugue; finally, a fugue by Wilhelm Friedemann Bach, with a newly composed prelude by "Mozart." It is worth observing that all the arrangements are scrupulously literal—pious, one might say—and that they include items from the Organ Trios, which we know were in van Swieten's position, as well as a fugue from the Art of Fugue, which we otherwise do not know for a fact to have been in van Swieten's collection. (Van Swieten's collection, by the way, also contained Handel's keyboard suites; C. P. E. Bach's sonatas and other key-

*Stage 2:* After faithful transcription, Mozart proceeded to stylistic imitation. The best-known example, and the only Bachian composition of this period that Mozart managed to complete, is the Prelude and Fugue in C Major, K.394/383a. This is the work that is accompanied by the famous letter to Nannerl, in which Mozart relates: "My dear Constanze is really the cause of this fugue's coming into the world. . . . Well, as she had often heard me play fugues out of my head, she asked me if I had ever written any down, and when I said I had not, she scolded me roundly for not recording some of my compositions in this most artistic and beautiful of all musical forms, and never ceased to entreat me until I wrote down a fugue for her."[29]

Two points are worth noting about this passage. First, Mozart claims that while he had "often" played "fugues out of my head," he had never "written any down." Apparently he had completely forgotten about K.401. Second, the fact that Mozart wrote this composition to please his wife has been taken by Stanley Sadie as an indication that Mozart himself was not particularly enthusiastic about fugal writing. Sadie comments: "It would . . . seem that the prospect of pleasing his fiancée and paying his respects to Van Swieten rather than any profound impact made by the music of Bach or Handel, lay behind the countless fugues which he started during 1782—started, but did not finish; for to Mozart these were nearer to technical experiments than to genuine artistic expression, so the spur to complete them was absent. (Almost everything he wrote for Constanze, incidentally, was left unfinished.)"[30]

It is worth remembering, however, that in his letter to Nannerl Mozart refers to fugue as "this most artistic and beautiful of all musical forms" ("das künstlichste und schönste in der Musick")—a characterization implying that

---

board pieces; sonatas and fugues by Domenico Scarlatti; keyboard pieces by Geminiani; and sonatas of Clementi. See Holschneider, "Die musikalische Bibliothek Gottfried van Swietens." Mozart no doubt got to know quite a few of these works as well.

29. Letter of 20 April 1782. *The Letters of Mozart and His Family,* 801; *Mozart Briefe und Aufzeichnungen,* vol.3, 202–3: "[Die] ursache daß diese fuge auf die Welt gekommen ist wirklich Meine liebe Konstanze. . . . weil sie mich nun öfters aus dem kopfe fugen spiellen gehört hat, so fragte sie mich ob ich noch keine aufgeschrieben hätte?—und als ich ihr Nein sagte.—so zankte sie mich recht sehr daß ich eben das künstlichste und schönste in der Musick nicht schreiben wollte; und gab mit bitten nicht nach, bis ich ihr eine fuge aufsezte, und so ward sie."

30. Sadie, "Mozart, Bach, and Counterpoint," 24.

EX. 7. *a*, K.394/2, subject.
*b*, BWV 846/2, subject

the composition of K.394 represented more than merely a wish to oblige Constanze or Van Swieten.

As for Mozart's fugue, it is clear that he derived the subject from the C-major fugue of the Well-Tempered Clavier, Book 1. In effect Mozart detached the four opening notes from the beginning of Bach's subject and appended them to the end (ex.7).

The fugue is an imitation; but perhaps it should more properly be considered an homage to J. S. Bach. As a composition, the work is less than altogether successful. Apart from the rather wooden, regular two-measure phrases throughout (a point already observed by Edward Lowinsky), the appoggiaturas of the countersubject are unprepared and unmotivated; they seem to have been introduced only for the sake of creating a dissonant "Bachian" effect.[31] Similarly, the later sequential chain of fourths, especially in the strettos in diminution, is quite awkward. In effect, while Mozart may have managed to capture the surface of Bach's fugue, he missed its essence.

*Stage 3:* Assimilation and synthesis. The ultimate artistic accomplishment of Mozart's 1782 encounter with Bach was to find a way to incorporate the stylistic vocabulary and technical complexity of Bach's music into the framework of his own personal instrumental idiom. This Mozart achieved by the end of 1782. He knew that he had made a decisive advance. On 28 December 1782 Mozart wrote to his father: "I should like to write a book, a short introduc-

---

31. Edward E. Lowinsky, "On Mozart's Rhythm," *Musical Quarterly* 42 (1956): 162–86, at pp.162–63; reprinted in *The Creative World of Mozart*, ed. Paul Henry Lang (New York: W. W. Norton & Co., 1963), 31–55, at pp.31–32.

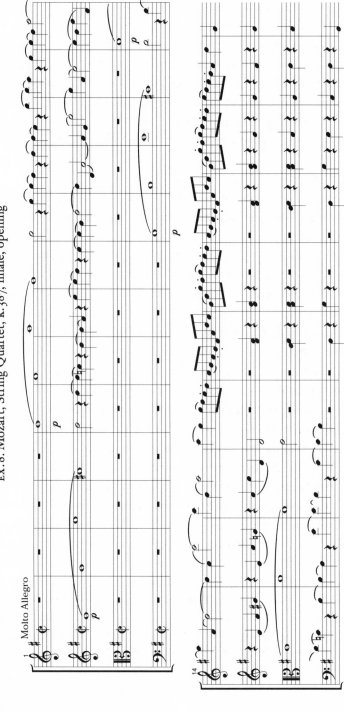

EX. 8. Mozart, String Quartet, K. 387, finale, opening

tion to music, illustrated by examples."[32] At just that time he was putting the finishing touches on the first of the six string quartets he would eventually publish and dedicate to Joseph Haydn: the Quartet in G, K.387, which bears the date "li 31 de decembre 1782" at the top of the autograph score. The G-major quartet is Mozart's first mature masterpiece in the genre of the string quartet. Within the previous six months Mozart had completed two other "watershed" masterpieces in his career: the Piano Concerto in A, K.414/385p, the first of the mature Viennese piano concerti, and *Die Entführung aus dem Serail*, the work that had preoccupied him for an entire year (from 30 July 1781). It is easy to imagine that when Mozart reflected on what he had achieved in these works he concluded that he had something of value to say on the subject of music. (So why not write a book?!)

What he had achieved in the G-major quartet—most spectacularly and famously so, in the last movement—was a reconciliation, a rapprochement, of the antithetical polyphonic and homophonic principles of the fugue and the sonata. I deliberately refrain from calling it a "synthesis"—it is not, strictly speaking, a synthesis, since the two idioms appear programmatically in stark alternation from section to section throughout the movement. But by introducing the two idioms into the same movement, Mozart demonstrated the effectiveness, the viability, the validity, of strict fugal procedure for the contemporary, classical style (ex. 8).

The principal lesson for Mozart of the encounter with the music of Bach through the stages of transcription, imitation, and assimilation was not only that it made available an enormous expansion of stylistic and technical resources. Most important, all of this Bachian armory was in the service of a profoundly deepened understanding of the nature of musical expression. Finally, as the G-major quartet had at least suggested, these resources had the capacity of being effectively subsumed within the prevailing contemporary instrumental idiom.

After 1782 Mozart made ever more natural, more self-confident use of the compositional resources he had appropriated from Bach. Contrapuntal sophistication and harmonic subtlety were henceforth *eine Selbstverständlichkeit*. The transparent and kaleidoscopically changing textures of even the most

---

32. *The Letters of Mozart and His Family*, 833; *Mozart Briefe und Aufzeichnungen*, vol.3, 246: "[I]ch hätte lust ein Buch—eine kleine Musicalische kritick mit Exemplen zu schreiben."

modest pieces, such as the miniature Divertimenti for Three Bassett Horns, K. 439b, are so exquisite and refined that they could, and should, serve as late-eighteenth-century instructive counterparts to Bach's three-part inventions, that is, as models of the Classical-era ideal of strict part writing (ex. 9).

Another striking example of what could be termed "classical counterpoint" is the opening theme of the Serenade in E-flat for Wind Instruments, K. 375, again with its iridescent transparency and understated, ever-changing, quasi-polyphonic dialog taking place below the theme (ex. 10).

Mozart continued to imitate Bach, that is, to challenge—and, if possible, surpass—J. S. Bach on his own terms: to indulge his own propensity (no doubt acquired from the example of Bach) for overt exhibitions of compositional bravado. The two most spectacular, no doubt, are the Dance Scene from the First Act finale of *Don Giovanni*, in which three orchestras play three dances simultaneously in three different meters, and the coda of the fourth movement of the "Jupiter" Symphony, in which five themes are presented in mutually invertible counterpoint. It is tempting to suggest that Mozart consciously derived the "Jupiter coda" from the example of Bach's permutation fugue. But I have not found any evidence that Mozart was familiar with any of Bach's strict permutation fugues. As for the Dance Scene from *Don Giovanni*, I know of no such tour de force involving conflicting meters in the music of Bach. What is most miraculous is that both escapades—the Dance Scene and the symphony coda—while challenging the technical and aesthetic limits and no doubt the intellectual capacities of the contemporary audience, manage nonetheless to remain within the basic stylistic context of the late eighteenth century.

That the stages of Mozart's Bach "reception"—transcription, imitation, assimilation/synthesis, and (if one is willing to accept my gloss on the "Jupiter" and *Don Giovanni* examples) transcendance—represent a conceptual, not a chronological, progression, is made clear by Mozart's journey to Leipzig in 1789. The visit precipitated a second systematic phase of largely derivative stylistic imitation. It was during this visit that Mozart heard Bach's motets: *Singet dem Herrn* for certain, probably *Jesu meine Freude*, and perhaps others as well. According to a famous anecdote reported by Friedrich Rochlitz in 1799:

> On the initiative of the late Doles, then cantor of the Thomas-Schule at Leipzig, the choir surprised Mozart with the performance of the double-chorus motet *Singet dem Herrn ein neues Lied* [BWV 225], by Sebastian Bach. . . . He was told

69

EX.10. Mozart, Serenade in E-flat for Wind Instruments, K.375, Movement 1, opening

that this School . . . possessed the complete collection of his motets and preserved them as a sort of sacred relic. "That's the spirit! That's fine!" he cried.
"Let's see them!" There was, however, no score of these songs; so he had the
parts given to him; and . . . Mozart sat himself down, with the parts all around
him . . . and, forgetting everything else, did not get up again until he had looked
through everything of Sebastian Bach's that was there. He requested a copy,
valued it very highly, and, if I am not very much mistaken, no one who knows
Bach's compositions and Mozart's *Requiem* will fail to recognize . . . the study,
the esteem, and the full comprehension of the spirit of the old contrapuntist
achieved by Mozart's versatile and unlimited genius.[33]

Bach's immediate influence upon Mozart's late vocal music is evident not
only in the fugal choruses of the Requiem but most notably, as is well known,
in the episode for the "armed men" from the Act 2 finale of *Die Zauberflöte*.
The music for this scene is set in the style of a Bach chorale prelude and even
uses the melody of the Lutheran chorale *Ach Gott vom Himmel sieh darein* as a
cantus firmus. Moreover, as Reinhold Hammerstein has observed, its counter-
points closely resemble elements from the movement "Gute Nacht, o Wesen"
from Bach's motet *Jesu Meine Freude*, BWV 227 (ex.11).[34]

I suspect that Mozart was inspired to set the scene in this fashion after study-
ing those parts for the "complete collection of [Bach's] motets" mentioned by
Rochlitz that were preserved in the Thomasschule; for among them were not
only the sources of *Singet dem Herrn* and *Jesu meine Freude* but also a set of
parts for Bach's chorale cantata *Ach Gott vom Himmel sieh darein*, BWV 2, whose
opening movement is set in motet style.

It was, in fact, not unusual at the time for motet-style choruses from Bach's
cantatas to be preserved together with the manuscripts of the motets proper.
Particularly pertinent in this respect is a mid-eighteenth-century score manuscript miscellany (SBB Am. B.12–14), copied in Berlin and belonging to the
collection of the Princess Anna Amalia—and thus surely available to Baron van
Swieten, too—that unites the opening chorus of *Ach, Gott vom Himmel* with
the equally motet-style opening chorus of *Aus tiefer Not schrei ich zu dir*, BWV
38, and the motet *Jesu meine Freude*, BWV 227.[35]

33. *Allgemeine Musikalische Zeitung* 1 (1799): 117. Translation in BR, 359–60.

34. Hammerstein, "Der Gesang der geharnischten Männer," 15–16.

35. See NBA III/1, KB, 94.

EX.11. *a*, Mozart, *Die Zauberflöte*, Act 2: Scene of the Armed Men, opening.
*b*, BWV 227/9. *Jesu meine Freude*: Gute Nacht, opening

At the end of Mozart's life the example and provocation of J. S. Bach make their appearance not only in the context of such major compositions as *Die Zauberflöte* and the Requiem, but even in the unlikely arena of a piece for a mechanical clock. The so-called Fantasy in F Minor, к.608, composed in March 1791, is in many respects Mozart's boldest effort at unabashed Bachian style imitation.[36] The piece's ritornello, with its heavy downbeat chords and contrasting dotted figures, seems to contain an allusion to the E-flat prelude from

36. The title for the work in Mozart's *Verzeichnüss* reads: *Ein OrgelStücke für eine Uhr.*

*Clavierübung* III, published in 1739, which Mozart surely got to know through Van Swieten (ex. 12).

The ritornello alternates here with a number of episodes, two of which are complete fugues that are based on the same theme and are studded with inversions, stretti, and harmonic, indeed, enharmonic audacities that propel the

EX.12. (*continued*)

first fugue of this F-minor composition into the key of F♯ minor, whereupon
the ritornello reappears in that key. Complementing the reference of the ritornello theme to that of Bach's *Clavierübung* prelude, Mozart's fugue theme, for
all the Bachian artifice of its ensuing treatment, has in fact been borrowed
from George Frideric Handel. It is effectively a condensation (or reduction)
of the double subject of the opening fugue from Handel's only authentic, pub-

76

EX. 13. a, Handel, Fugue in G Minor, HWV 605, opening.
b, K. 608, mm. 13–15

lished collection of such pieces, the *Six Fugues or Voluntarys for the Organ or Harpsichord* (ex.13).[37]

More important than his witty thematic allusions to both Bach and Handel is the fact that Mozart seems to have striven here not only to emulate, but to trump, the structural conception underlying the prelude and fugue from the *Clavierübung*. Bach's prelude and fugue are, typically, autonomous, self-contained compositions: in fact, in the original edition of the *Clavierübung* they are placed, respectively, at the beginning and end of the compilation, and thus emphatically separated from each other by no fewer than twenty-five intervening compositions. Mozart, in contrast, by inserting the fugues as episodes between the ritornelli of his Fantasy, has managed to combine the major premises of Bach's prelude—the ritornello form and regal character—with the idea of a multisectional fugue that is the central premise, and the hallmark, of Bach's grandiose concluding work into a single continuous composition.

The Fantasy, then, not unlike the finale of the G-major string quartet K.387, programmatically unites within a single movement two contrasting compositional models or principles—this time both intimately associated with the figure of Johann Sebastian Bach, and both, at least since Bach, traditionally regarded as polar antitheses: those of prelude and fugue. That Mozart saw fit to do this by means of a fugue theme stolen from Handel is all the more piquant.

Of course, the whole notion of such combinatorial virtuosity—the synthesis and unification of opposites, the idea of a universal music as constituting a musical universe—all this, too, is an essential part of Johann Sebastian Bach's legacy to Wolfgang Amade Mozart.[38]

\* \* \*

Mozart's encounter with Johann Sebastian Bach was, in the end, energized not so much by the sense of *discovery*—of the archaic, the alien, the Other—as by

37. Handel's collection, published by Walsh, as the composer's *Troisième Ouvrage*, appeared around 1735, i.e., virtually contemporaneously with Bach's *Clavierübung* III. The individual compositions, however, were evidently composed in the second decade of the eighteenth century: the G-minor is thought to have been composed ca.1711, the remaining five fugues ca.1717/18.

38. On this point see my essay "On Bach's Universality," in Robert L. Marshall, *The Music of Johann Sebastian Bach: The Sources, the Style, the Significance* (New York: Schirmer Books, 1989), 65–79.

a sense of *recognition:* the recognition in Bach's music of the successful fulfillment and embodiment of many of his own artistic impulses. In the uncompromising, intricate stylistic and expressive musical idiom of Johann Sebastian Bach, Mozart had not discovered the Other; he had come to recognize a hitherto largely unacknowledged and undeveloped part of his own musical personality. It was a matter, if anything, of *self*-discovery.

# Bachian Affinities
# in Beethoven

## William Kinderman

The very first printed notice about Beethoven, from C. F. Cramer's *Magazin der Musik* in 1783, stresses the importance of J. S. Bach's music for the young musician at Bonn:

> Louis van Betthoven, son of the tenor singer mentioned, a boy of eleven years and of most promising talent. He plays the clavier very skillfully and with power, reads at sight very well, and—to put it in a nutshell—he plays chiefly *The Well-Tempered Clavier* of Sebastian Bach, which Herr Neefe has put into his hands. Whoever knows this collection of preludes and fugues in all the keys— which might almost be called the *non plus ultra* of our art—will know what this means. . . . This youthful genius is deserving of help to enable him to travel. He would surely become a second Wolfgang Amadeus Mozart were he to continue as he has begun.[1]

This description, penned by Beethoven's teacher in Bonn, Christian Gottlob Neefe, points to the formative influence of Bach's music on Neefe's brilliant pupil. Like Haydn and Mozart before him, Beethoven was to be exposed during his first Vienna years to works of Handel and J. S. Bach at the musical gatherings of the venerable connoisseur Baron Gottfried van Swieten, who had developed his taste for Bach in Berlin before moving to the Austrian capital. Unlike his predecessors, however, the young Beethoven pursued a musical direction that was already shaped by the Leipzig master. From an early stage

---

A longer, German version of this study appears in *Bach und die Nachwelt*, ed. Michael Heinemann and Hans-Joachim Hinrichsen (Laaber: Laaber, 1997).

1. *Thayer's Life of Beethoven*, ed. Eliot Forbes (Princeton: Princeton University Press, 1964) [hereafter Thayer-Forbes], 66. The spelling "Betthoven" appears in the original source. Beethoven was actually twelve years old at the time in question.

Bach's music counterbalanced for Beethoven the pervasive presence of the galant, that elegant but superficial manner that had threatened to submerge Mozart's originality during the 1770s. So thorough was Beethoven's assimilation of Bach, in fact, that Erwin Ratz was able to base an illuminating study of musical form precisely on the comparison of Bach's inventions and fugues with Beethoven's sonatas and quartets.[2]

Studies of J. S. Bach's influence on Beethoven have emphasized the later periods of his career, after 1813, in connection with Beethoven's growing interest in fugue and other aspects of Baroque style.[3] However, Beethoven's early acquaintance with Bach's celebrated work for Frederick the Great of Prussia, the Musical Offering of 1747, seems to be reflected in his *2 Präludien durch die 12 Dur-Tonarten für Klavier oder Orgel*, pieces stemming from the 1780s and revised in 1789, although published only in 1803 as op. 39.[4] Beethoven's cyclical plan of modulations rises through the circle of fifths from C major to C♯ major and then falls through the flat keys, reaching D♭ major before returning to C major. There were, to be sure, various historical models for such modulating preludes "per tonus"; the best known was probably Bach's perpetual canon, in the Musical Offering, on the royal theme "Ascendente Modulatione ascendat Gloria Regis," in which continual ascent of the canon symbolizes the endlessly rising glory of the king. The modulations in Bach's canon proceed not by fifths but by rising whole steps; after six repetitions the original key is thus reattained an octave higher. In his stimulating 1979 study *Gödel, Escher, Bach: An Eternal Golden Braid*, Douglas R. Hofstadter described this "endlessly rising canon" as one model for M. C. Escher's paradoxical depictions of the infinite in his graphic prints from the 1960s.[5] The young Beethoven was not unaffected by

2. Erwin Ratz, *Einführung in die musikalische Formenlehre* (Vienna: Universal, 1968).

3. See, e.g., Martin Zenck, *Die Bach-Rezeption des Späten Beethoven: Zum Verhaltnis von Musikhistoriographie und Rezeptionsgeschichtesschreibung der "Klassik"* (Stuttgart: Franz Steiner Verlag, 1986). Also see Warren Kirkendale, *Fugue and Fugato in Rococo and Classical Chamber Music* (Durham: Duke University Press, 1979), 212-25, 246-47, 268-71, and Ernst Fritz Schmid, "Beethovens Bachkenntnis," *Neues Beethoven Jahrbuch* 5 (1933): 64-83.

4. For a recent discussion of this work, see Jurij Cholopow, "2 Präludien für Klavier/Orgel op. 39," in *Beethoven: Interpretationen seiner Werke*, vol. 1, ed. Albrecht Riethmüller, Carl Dahlhaus, and Alexander Ringer (Laaber: Laaber, 1994), 309-10.

5. See Hofstadter, *Gödel, Escher, Bach: An Eternal Golden Braid* (New York: Vintage, 1989), 10.

this esoteric side of Bach's legacy, although its full impact surfaces only much later, in works of his last decade.

If Beethoven's interest in Bach ultimately centered on counterpoint and fugue, his Bachian affinities are also reflected in aspects of his rhythm, figuration, musical character, and formal procedures, as is perhaps most clearly seen in some of his piano sonatas. After his arrival in Vienna in 1792, Beethoven gained access to a wide selection of J. S. Bach's keyboard, chamber, and vocal music, which was then available in the form of copies as well as a few printed scores. He himself actively encouraged the growing dissemination of Bach's music through publication of new editions. The emergence of new music publications at the turn of the nineteenth century coincided with both the rediscovery of Bach and the rising fame of Beethoven. Early issues of the *Intelligenz-Blatt* of the *Allgemeine musikalische Zeitung*, published by Breitkopf and Härtel beginning in 1798, included appeals for funds to assist Regina Susanna Bach, J. S. Bach's last surviving child. In his letter to the firm dated 22 April 1801, Beethoven expressed disappointment at the amount of money raised and offered to publish a work for her benefit.[6] In 1800 another of Beethoven's publishers, the Bureau de Musique in Leipzig, a partnership of Hoffmeister and Kühnel, began to issue the *Oeuvre complettes de Jean Sebastien Bach*, an edition that Beethoven possessed and from which he copied extracts from the Chromatic Fantasy and Fugue in 1810, to be discussed below.

Bach's music was also disseminated through such publications as Johann Philipp Kirnberger's *Die Kunst des Reinen Satzes* and Friedrich Wilhelm Marpurg's *Abhandlung von der Fuge*, treatises that Beethoven possessed in editions from 1793 and 1801 respectively. As Ratz has observed, one challenge to assessing the impact of Bach's works on Beethoven lies in their role as models of compositional technique, a role to which Bach himself alluded in the preface to the 1723 manuscript of his inventions: "An Upright Guide . . . whereby good inventions are not only offered, but also are to be properly executed . . . to convey in addition a strong foretaste for composition" ("Auffrichtige Anleitung . . . Anbey auch zugleich gute Inventiones nicht alleine zu bekommen, sondern auch selbige wohl durchzuführen . . . und darneben einen starken Vorschmack

6. Cf. especially Gottfried Christoph Härtel's letter to Beethoven of 21 May 1801 in *Letters to Beethoven & Other Correspondence*, vol. 1, trans. and ed. Theodore Albrecht (Lincoln: University of Nebraska Press, 1996), L.34.

von der Composition zu überkommen"). In Bach's three-part Sinfonias, Ratz finds models for Beethoven's development procedures in his sonata forms, arguing that "it was not only the unique synthesis of polyphonic and harmonic thought that Beethoven so admired in Bach's music. He also found essential homophonic formal principles in Bach. Inasmuch as Beethoven drew on precisely these formal elements and, recognizing their special viability, developed them further—rather than adopting various other formal tendencies in Haydn and Mozart, which were later cultivated above all by Brahms—we can speak in this regard of a direct continution of the Bachian legacy."[7]

The parallel formal principles discussed by Ratz remind us of the magnitude of the subject of Beethoven's Bach reception, and of the difficulty of doing justice to the topic in a single essay. One might distinguish here between procedural or structural assimilation on the one hand, and stylistic influence on the other. As Ratz observes, the former category involves the specific means of artistic realization of the otherwise vague goal of organic unity: a coherent elaboration of musical ideas through motivic, rhythmic, harmonic, and tonal means, while balance is maintained between repose and movement, exposition and development. A fundamental means of such musical development lies in a compression of structural units, so that for instance what had occupied one full measure is telescoped into half-measures or quarter-measures, thereby generating forward drive and an increasing concentration of motivic content. This procedure is clearly demonstrated in the opening section of Bach's ingenious Two-Part Invention in C Major, BWV 772, among many other examples. In Beethoven, this crucial resource of structural compression is sometimes called "fragmentation"—Alfred Brendel has more suitably termed it "foreshortening" and described it as *the* driving force of his sonata forms and a basic principle of his musical thought."[8] The almost obsessive use of such foreshortening in a work like the opening Allegro of Beethoven's first Sonata in F Minor, op. 2, no. 1 (1795) bears a debt to Bach, although the actual thematic material owes nothing to him.

In so internalizing Bach's "solidity" or "Festigkeit," as he put it in his letter of July 1819, cited below, Beethoven enriched and fortified the dramatic music

7. Ratz, *Einführung in die musikalische Formenlehre*, 21–22.

8. Brendel, "Form and Psychology in Beethoven's Piano Sonatas," in his *Musical Thoughts and Afterthoughts* (Princeton: Princeton University Press, 1976), 43.

idiom of the late eighteenth century. Harold Bloom's concept of "anxiety of influence" seems hardly appropriate here.[9] It seems rather that Bach took on an important enabling function for the young Beethoven, helping him to distinguish his architectural approach to composition from the powerful, potentially overwhelming models of Haydn and Mozart. Striking nevertheless, in view of Bloom's theory of artistic competition, is Beethoven's lifelong tendency to verbally extol Handel and Mozart more than Bach and Haydn. In its deterministic, goal-directed aesthetic, Beethoven's music is often closer in spirit to the latter than the former, yet this very closeness may have discouraged conscious acknowledgment.

The stylistic influence of Bach on Beethoven is felt particularly in the latter's works for piano. Often we can discern a relation to that Bachian masterpiece, the playing of which established Beethoven's reputation as a prodigy: the Well-Tempered Clavier, especially Book 1. Jürgen Uhde observed, for instance, that Beethoven's Sonata in F♯ Major, op. 78 (1809) displays an intimately lyrical character reminiscent of Bach's pieces in this key in the Well-Tempered Clavier.[10] In the "Grande Sonate" in E♭ Major, op. 7 (1797), on the other hand, a kinship with Bach surfaces in the central episode of the gracious rondo finale. The main theme of this rondo unfolds with expressive appoggiaturas above a pedal point on the dominant, conveying an intimately lyrical, heartfelt character. Whereas the first and third episodes of the form transform motives from this main theme into animated dialogue, the central episode releases a drastic contrast—a loud and turbulent C-minor idiom recalling Bach's prelude in this key from Book 1 of the Well-Tempered Clavier (ex. 1a and 1b). The similarity of these passages derives from their use of a relentless ostinato figure in duple time, with the figuration in Beethoven's sonata notated in thirty-second notes instead of sixteenths. Like Bach, Beethoven stresses turn-figures in his figuration, but he also superimposes heavy chords and syncopated accents on the toccata-like texture in C minor.

Beethoven incorporates this stylistic allusion as a dramatic element within

9. Several of Bloom's books have elaborated his theory of literary influence, especially *The Anxiety of Influence* (New York: Oxford University Press, 1973), *A Map of Misreading* (New York: Oxford University Press, 1975), and, most recently, *The Western Canon* (New York: Harcourt Brace, 1994).

10. Uhde, *Beethovens Klaviermusik*, vol. 3 (Stuttgart: Reclam, 1974), 226.

EX.1. *a*, J. S. Bach, Prelude in C Minor, Well-Tempered Clavier, Book 1.
  *b*, Beethoven, Sonata in E♭ Major, op. 7, beginning of central episode in
    finale.
  *c*, Beethoven, Sonata in E♭ Major, op. 7, coda of finale

his sonata. The role of the C-minor episode goes beyond its immediate context, since this is precisely the passage that Beethoven resolves into graceful accents in the very last moments of the rondo (ex. 1c). Beethoven prepares the coda with an ethereal vision of the main rondo theme lifted into E major. In his ensuing farewell to the listener, he then resolves the turbulent C minor idiom reminiscent of Bach's prelude into a gently understated, transparent E♭ major, transforming strife into grace.

In the finale of a later piano sonata—the Sonata in F Major, op. 54 (1804)—Beethoven expanded this kind of stylistic allusion to Bach to an entire movement. Here, as in op. 7, the reference is to a toccata-like idiom employing a *perpetuum mobile* rhythm of sixteenth notes. The texture is confined to two voices in imitative counterpoint; the main subject begins with an arpeggiation through the octave followed by a linear, sequential pattern, consisting in Beethoven's case of a chain of rising sixths. Ratz compares this movement to Bach's larger organ works and solo suites, but a closer point of reference is to the E-minor fugue from Book 1 of the Well-Tempered Clavier—the only fugue in the entire collection in two voices.[11] Characteristically, Beethoven transforms his model. Whereas Bach's subject descends, Beethoven's ascends; and Beethoven's subject replaces the chromaticism of Bach's with a configuration of smooth diatonic rising sixths, marked *dolce*.

This frequently underestimated sonata shows a remarkable assimilation of Bach's style into the more dramatic context of Beethoven's classical musical language. Opus 54 is the first of Beethoven's larger sonatas to compress the formal plan into a pair of movements. Its sonata-form finale unfolds with an irresistible momentum in long ascending lines punctuated by syncopated pedal notes. If the two-voice texture is reminiscent of Bach, the dramatic power is unmistakably Beethovenian. In the development, Beethoven inverts the ascending linear motion so that it sinks chromatically into the depths of the bass, preparing a modulation into C minor. The coda accelerates the perpetual motion in a furious *piu allegro* that sweeps all before it. We can discern in this rhythmic drive a key to the relation between the two strongly contrasting movements of op. 54. The minuet with which the first movement began had proceeded in halting fashion, stopping every two or four measures in cadences set off by rests, but the assertive contrasting theme of that movement infused

11. Ratz, *Einführung in die musikalische Formenlehre*, 148.

the music with an energy that in the finale becomes an all-encompassing force. The discovery, integration, and celebration of this rhythmic energy is a guiding idea of the sonata as a whole. In op. 54, as in the finale of op. 7, Beethoven's stylistic transformation of Bach affects the culmination of the work as a whole.

\* \* \*

Assessing compositional influence as manifested in thematic similarities between works is more intricate. One striking example is the kinship between Bach's setting of "Es ist vollbracht" in the St. John Passion and Beethoven's paired phrases in F♯ minor for piano and cello near the beginning of the development of the first movement of his Cello Sonata in A Major, op. 69, composed in 1807–8. To be sure, these phrases in op. 69 are related to the second half of the initial phrase of the movement, heard in the unaccompanied cello, whereas Beethoven's acquaintance with the St. John Passion, then still unpublished, is not documented. Still, as Peter Schleuning and others have observed, this thematic similarity has a broader context and also calls to mind the head of the *Arioso dolente* in the finale of Beethoven's Piano Sonata in A♭ Major, op. 110 (1821).[12] It is striking how Beethoven assigns in op. 69 one of Bach's best-known melodies for the gamba to its historical successor: the cello. In the cello sonata, the thematic allusion remains latent until the isolation of the Bachian phrase in the minor mode in the development. This passage may be heard as deepening the expressive context of the entire movement, although perhaps not so unequivocally as in the piano sonata, in which a relation to baroque style is more strongly felt.

Another somewhat elusive area of influence concerns the use of formal types, such as the sarabande-like themes Beethoven employed for his variation movements in the "Archduke" Trio in B♭ Major, op. 97 (1811), and in the Piano Sonata in E Major, op. 109 (1820).[13] One model for these themes may have been

12. For a recent discussion of this relationship as well as of other thematic similarities to J. S. Bach in the music of Beethoven's middle period, see Schleuning, "Cellosonate A-Dur op. 69," in Riethmüller, *Beethoven: Interpretationen seiner Werke*, 519–20. On the kinship between Bach's St. John Passion and Beethoven's *Arioso dolente* in op. 110, see, among others, Denis Matthews, *Beethoven* (London: Dent, 1985), 115; Martin Geck, *Johann Sebastian Bach. Johannespassion* BWV 245 (Munich: Fink, 1991), 93; and Wilfrid Mellers, *Beethoven and the Voice of God* (New York: Oxford University Press, 1983), 299–32.

13. In his *Vortragslehre*, Carl Czerny wrote about the variation finale of op. 109 that the "whole movement was in the style of Handel and Bach" ("der ganze Satz im Style *Handels und Seb:*

the Aria from Bach's "Goldberg" Variations, but the relation remains generalized rather than specific. On the other hand, in his Variations in C Minor for Piano, WoO 80 (1806), Beethoven came very close to the Baroque chaconne. But while Bach may have exerted influence, other composers, especially Handel, may have been even more influential. This work employs a short, eight-measure theme with a chromatically descending ground bass. Its clear kinship to Baroque practice may have seemed a defect rather than a virtue to Beethoven, who seriously underrated the work, referred to it disparagingly, and failed to assign it an opus number.

The influence of Bach on Beethoven generally coincides, as it had with Mozart, with an enhanced contrapuntal density of the musical language. In Beethoven's case this tendency can be traced over decades of his life, especially after 1810. In the "Quartetto Serioso" in F Minor, op. 95 (1810), he incorporates a slow movement in D major, marked *Allegretto ma non troppo*, which contains extended fugal passages based on a chromatic subject. In the "Archduke" Trio in B♭ Major, written the following year, he places an uncanny chromatic canon at the beginning of the trio—a passage exploring those spaces between steps of the diatonic major scale that were passed over lightly by the scherzo. In a recent study of the sketches for the trio contained in the Landsberg 11 sketchbook (housed in Kraków, Poland), Seow-Chin Ong associates the "fluid and meandering chromaticism . . . and its attendant harmonic ambiguities . . . with Beethoven's apparent renewed interest in Bach, for Landsberg 11 contains extensive excerpts from the *Chromatic Fantasy and Fugue* that he had copied out, apparently from a slightly corrupt print."[14] Not only did Beethoven copy out parts of the fantasy written in dissonant free arpeggios; he also wrote down the fugue's entire exposition. His interest in this Bachian work may have been connected to his preoccupation with keyboard cadenzas and fantasies around 1809 as well as to an enhanced interest in fugue and fugato. It is in the sonatas from 1814 and after, however, that the expanded contrapuntal dimension be-

---

*Bach's*"). See Czerny, *Über den richtigen Vortrag der sämtlichen Beethoven'schen Klavierwerke*, ed. with a commentary by Paul Badura-Skoda (Vienna: Universal, 1963), 60.

14. "Beethoven's 'Archduke' Trio: The Sketches for the Scherzo," unpublished paper read at the annual meeting of the American Musicological Society, Montreal, 1993. A more detailed discussion is contained in Ong's forthcoming edition of the Landsberg 11 sketchbook. The "slightly corrupt print" was the Leipzig "Kühnel'sche Ausgabe," as was pointed out by Gustav Nottebohm in *Zweite Beethoveniana* (Leipzig, 1887), 286.

comes a mainstay of Beethoven's art. This contrapuntal density is an essential ingredient of his late style, which absorbs the polyphonic richness characteristic of Bach into a dramatic, contrast-laden idiom, more progressive than archaic in cast.

In accordance with this stylistic synthesis, Beethoven's later use of such counterpoint is often innovative and exploratory, standing in flexible relation to the musical form. Canon and fugue are treated less as ends in themselves than as means to an end. A good example of this practice is the canonic passage leading to the recapitulation of the first movement from the Piano Sonata in E Minor, op. 90. The second half of the development (mm. 113 ff.) employs an accompanimental texture outlining broken chords in the right hand, while a figure drawn from the opening theme is intensified with *sforzandi* in the left hand (ex. 2). Especially fascinating is how the musical content of m. 130 — where Beethoven changes the key signature to one sharp, indicating E minor — is treated in the ensuing canonic passage to allow the recapitulation to emerge. This measure already contains the essence of the recapitulation in its second and third beats, in particular in the third descent from G to E in the high register. After three repetitions (m. 131) this figure is isolated and stressed dynamically in the next measure, with an imitation an octave lower. Then a series of canonic mutations elongates the figure in three successive rhythmic augmentations, and its relationship with the principal theme gradually becomes clear. The close stretto at the unison (mm. 138–41) stresses the pitch level of the imminent recapitulation; in performance, these measures are difficult to bring out effectively, on account of their dense texture, as the motif continues to turn onto itself. Finally, the stretto expands across other registers and yields to the recapitulation (m. 144). There is no cadence; harmonically, this entire static passage has remained on the tonic. The rapid sixteenth-note figuration of the development has proven against all expectations to belong to the head of the principal theme. Instead of defining a single structural moment, the recapitulation represents a process that extends over the eighteen measures preceding the literal point of recapitulation.

This example illustrates the dynamic use of contrapuntal process that is so characteristic of the later Beethoven, and in relation to which he defined his posture vis-à-vis Bach. In a letter of 29 July 1819 to his patron and student the Archduke Rudolph, he characteristically praised the superior "solidity" (*Festigkeit*) of the older art of Handel and Sebastian Bach, while also stressing both the "refinement of our [modern] virtues that has advanced matters" and the

EX. 2. Beethoven, Sonata in E Minor, op. 90, end of development to recapitulation of first movement, mm. 124–46

need for "freedom and progress . . . in the world of art as in the whole of creation."[15] There is abundant evidence that Beethoven went against the grain of public taste in his cultivation of fugue in his later years. In particular, the fugal finales of works like the Cello Sonata in D Major, op. 102, no. 2 (1815) and the "Hammerklavier" Sonata in B♭ Major, op. 106 (1818) came under criticism for being overly intricate or labored. An 1824 reviewer of the Cello Sonata, probably Adolf Bernhard Marx, complained about the fugue: "How much we would

15. Thayer-Forbes, 741–42.

rather have heard another movement—a Beethovenian finale!—in place of this fugue. It would be therefore desirable that Beethoven not exploit fugue in such a willful manner, since his great genius is naturally lifted above every form." [16] Another reviewer compared Beethoven's accessible and popular Septet, op. 20, to the difficult "Hammerklavier" Sonata, to the detriment of the latter, stating: "It is strange, that Beethoven declared this work [the septet op. 20] to be one of his least successful. For even if its dimensions are somewhat broad, it is infinitely richer in true beauty than many of his later works, for instance the grand sonata, op. 106." [17]

More evidence of negative response from Beethoven's contemporaries comes in relation to the *Große Fuge*, op. 133, the original finale of the Quartet in B♭ Major, op. 130—a colossal movement from 1825 that Anton Schindler dubbed "the greatest monster of all quartet music" ("das Monstrum aller Quartett-Musik").

This complex, multisectional finale combines rigorous fugal procedures with aspects of variation technique and incorporates an elaborate preface or "Ouverture," which presents the main themes in reverse order. For all its audacious originality, the *Große Fuge* was described by Warren Kirkendale as Beethoven's Art of Fugue, as a compendium of fugal devices indebted to J. S. Bach and also inspired in part by one of Beethoven's teachers from his early Vienna years, Johann Georg Albrechtsberger. [18] The technical and interpretive difficulties of the *Große Fuge* equal or exceed those of Beethoven's other ambitious fugal finales: as is well known, in the end he decided, at the urgings of Karl Holz and the publisher Matthias Artaria, to write a substitute finale for the quartet. Noteworthy in this respect is Beethoven's lifelong high respect for

16. *Ludwig van Beethoven: Die Werke im Spiegel seiner Zeit—Gesammelte Konzertberichte und Rezensionen bis 1830*, ed. Stefan Kunze (Laaber: Laaber, 1987), 344. The original German text reads as follows: "Wie viel lieber hätten wir statt dieser Fuge einen andern Satz, ein Beethovensches Finale gehört! Es bleibt daher zu wünschen, daß Beethoven die Fuge nicht so absichtlich ergreife, da sein großes Genie ja über jede Form erhaben ist."

17. *Ludwig van Beethoven: Die Werke im Spiegel seiner Zeit*, 21: "Es ist sonderbar, daß Beethoven gerade dieses Werk fuer eines seiner wenigstgelungenen erklaert haben soll. Denn obwohl in der Anlage etwas reit, ist es doch unendlich viel reicher an wahren Schönheiten, als manche seiner späteren Werke, z.B. die große Sonate Opus 106."

18. See Kirkendale, "The 'Great Fugue' Op. 133: Beethoven's 'Art of the Fugue,'" *Acta musicologica* 35 (1963): 14–24.

Bach's fugues, which were not always so well regarded in the early nineteenth century, but which were often cultivated in the same milieu where Beethoven's music was performed. In 1809 Johann Friedrich Reichardt wrote about the role of Bach and Handel in the musical circle of the Baroness Dorothea von Ertmann and her occasional instructor Wilhelm Karl Rust; both keyboard players were appreciated by Beethoven, who once enthusiastically described Ertmann as his "dear, valued Dorothea-Cäcilia." During the following years, Ertmann received special praise for her performances of Beethoven's Sonata in E Minor, op. 90; she also received the dedication of Beethoven's Sonata in A Major, op. 101. In a letter from 1810, Rust commented about the performances of the Baroness: "She always makes music entirely as I imagine it. Either she plays me a Beethoven sonata that I select, or I play her favorite fugues by Handel and Bach." [19]

In this connection we may consider a discussion between Beethoven and his violinist friend Karl Holz from the end of December 1825, in which the topic turned to fugues. Only Holz's comments have been preserved, but the gist of Beethoven's replies may be surmised from the flow of the conversation:

> A fugue seems to me like a building that is constructed symmetrically according to all the rules of architecture; I admire it, but it will never delight me.
>
> ———
>
> I mean here the normal fugues.
>
> ———
>
> Ordinarily they are treated in a dry fashion; I'm speaking about these [fugues]; I can't stand them.
>
> ———
>
> I still haven't heard a fugue by S. Bach well played.[20]

It seems clear from the context that Beethoven took issue with Holz's dismissal of fugue as a dry and sterile affair and cited J. S. Bach's fugues as a counterexample. In his own use of fugue in his later works, Beethoven undertook to infuse this rich compositional resource with new poetic meaning and dramatic significance. As he put it on another occasion: "It is no challenge to write a fugue; in my student days I wrote dozens of them. But fantasy must also re-

19. Cited by Zenck, *Die Bach-Rezeption*, 152.

20. *Ludwig van Beethovens Konversationshefte*, vol. 8, ed. Karl-Heinz Köhler and Grita Herre (Leipzig: VEB Deutscher Verlag für Musik, 1981), 224.

ceive its due, and nowadays a different and really poetic aspect must be brought to the venerable form."[21]

How did the aging Beethoven distinguish his own fugal idioms from the Baroque models offered above all by Handel and Bach? In the letter from July 1819 to the Archduke Rudolph, he coins the term "artistic unification" (*Kunstvereinigung*) in connection with his intensive assimilation of these predecessors. Interesting in this respect is Beethoven's Fugue in D Major for String Quintet, op. 137 (1817), sketches for which are juxtaposed with excerpts drawn from Marpurg's *Abhandlung von der Fuge* (Berlin, 1753–54), and two passages each copied from Bach's Art of Fugue and from the B♭-minor fugue from Book 1 of the Well-Tempered Clavier. As Richard Kramer has observed, the sketches for op. 137 are found in association with fugal entries in D minor that are related to the Ninth Symphony, as well as with work on an arrangement for string quartet of the B-minor fugue from Book 1 of the Well-Tempered Clavier.[22]

The intensity of Beethoven's engagement with Bach during this period even surpasses Mozart's preoccupation with the Leipzig master beginning in 1782, when Baron van Swieten engaged Mozart to arrange Bach's keyboard fugues for strings. Beethoven's assimilation of Bach after 1814 represents a climactic development in the reception of the Baroque master's music: it is a process centered not on historical revival and emulation, as is often the case with Mendelssohn or Schumann, but involves a new stylistic synthesis. In his best works, Beethoven achieves a rare balance between the "direct continuation of the Bachian legacy" identified by Ratz and the self-conscious striving for artistic innovation characteristic of Romanticism.

Immediately after composing op. 137, Beethoven tackled the largest of all his piano sonatas, the "Hammerklavier" in B♭ Major, op. 106. As in two of his sonatas of preceding years, the Cello Sonata in C Major, op. 102, no. 1, and the Piano Sonata in A Major, op. 101, he incorporates here an elaborate transition to the finale—a transition suggesting a mysterious search for a viable continuation to the narrative sequence of movements. In both sonatas, this quest involves a *Rückblick*, a reminiscence of the opening movement, seen in a new

21. Thayer-Forbes, 692 (translation amended).

22. See Richard Kramer, "Fuge für Streichquintett op. 137," in *Beethoven: Interpretationen seiner Werke*, vol. 2, 269–72.

light. Such fantasy-like transitions enhance the impact of the finale, which now often becomes the most extended and weighty movement of the cycle. Polyphony is conspicuous in these finales: in op. 101, fugue comprises the development section of the sonata form, whereas in op. 102, no. 2, it shapes the entire movement, giving the finale the weight needed to balance the earlier movements.

In the "Hammerklavier," Beethoven crowns the narrative sequence of movements with a grand fugue that is exhaustive in developing the main subject—a subject linked in turn to the principal theme of the first movement and to the motivic descending thirds so important throughout the sonata. Before unveiling the fugue subject, he incorporates a largo transition offering glimpses of possible musical continuations, each of which are presented parenthetically and then abruptly discontinued. In this slow introduction to the finale, Beethoven first distills the intervallic basis of the whole sonata, reducing the music to a fundamental, underlying level of content consisting solely of the chain of falling thirds in the bass, accompanied by soft, hesitant chords in the treble. The chain of thirds is interrupted three times by brief visions of contrapuntal music, the last of which is most obviously Bachian in character (ex. 3). This allegro excerpt, with its driving syncopated rhythm, imitative counterpoint, and spidery figuration, suggests an energetic, toccata-like idiom, but the passage is broken off after five measures. As in the transition to the choral finale of the Ninth Symphony, there is a search towards new compositional possibilities, with the clear implication that Baroque counterpoint is transcended by the creation of a new contrapuntal style embodied in the revolutionary fugal finale of the sonata. Nevertheless, there is evidence that the Bb-major fugue from Book 2 of the Well-Tempered Clavier was connected to the genesis of the fugal finale from op. 106.

Martin Zenck has suggested that "the reconciled stylistic antithesis of fantasy and fugue" embodied in Beethoven's largo transition and fugal finale in op. 106 is indebted to Bach's Chromatic Fantasy and Fugue, BWV 903, parts of which, as we have noted, Beethoven copied out in 1810.[23] This parallel should not, however, be overstated. The chain of falling motivic thirds or fugal excerpts in the transition of the "Hammerklavier" has no counterpart in the Chromatic Fantasy and Fugue. These parenthetical excerpts rather seem "to

23. See Zenck, *Die Bach-Rezeption*, 199–219, esp. 218.

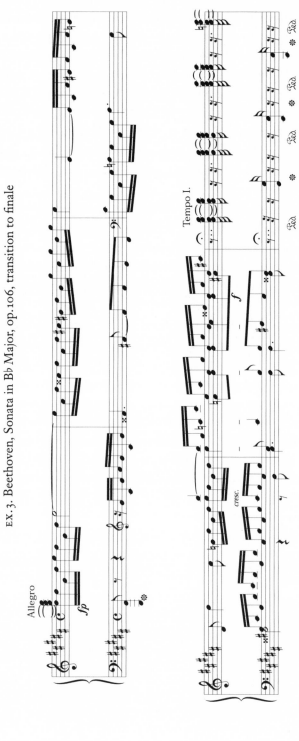

EX. 3. Beethoven, Sonata in Bb Major, op. 106, transition to finale

evoke some imaginary fugal moment from the past," in the words of Richard Kramer.[24] It is characteristic of Beethoven's evocations of Bach and other earlier styles that such references are assimilated into a progressive context, whereby older procedures are infused with "a different and really poetic aspect."

An outstanding example of this process is offered by Beethoven's penultimate sonata, op.110 in A♭ major. A. B. Marx, in his laudatory review of the sonata in 1824, observed that the fugue in the finale "has to be studied next to the richest by Bach and Handel." Marx also recognized how Beethoven's treatment departed from that of his predecessors and concluded: "This is a Beethovenian fugue. Look here, how one learns art and then leaves it behind through a liberated spiritual striving."[25] The dualistic finale contains an unusual double pairing of *Arioso dolente* and fugue, involving a tension-filled relation of complementary yet diametrically opposed modalities. Whereas the lament is laden with an expression of suffering reminiscent of the Agnus Dei from the *Missa solemnis*, the fugue is promising and affirmative, suggesting a kinship with the Dona nobis pacem, with which it shares a similar thematic outline of rising perfect fourths. The first fugue cannot be sustained, however; it is broken off on the dominant of A♭, before Beethoven reinterprets this pivotal sonority as a German augmented-sixth chord, casting the music into the remote key of G minor for the second and most despairing presentation of the *Arioso dolente*.

The interweaving of Baroque forms in op.110 offers one of Beethoven's most fascinating essays in which an evocation of older styles is assimilated into a narrative design with modernistic connotations. The beginning of the arioso theme has been compared to "Es ist vollbracht" from Bach's St. John Passion, as noted earlier; and Paul Badura-Skoda has recently identified an apparent "unconscious reminiscence" near the end of the first arioso of Bach's E♭-minor prelude from Book 1 of the Well-Tempered Clavier.[26] The second arioso, on the

---

24. Kramer, "Between Cavatina and Ouverture: Opus 130 and the Voices of Narrative," *Beethoven Forum*, vol.1 (Lincoln: University of Nebraska Press), 172.

25. This review, from the *Berliner allgemeine musikalische Zeitung* 1 (1824): 87–90, has been reprinted in *Ludwig van Beethoven: Die Werke im Spiegel seiner Zeit*, 368–74 (the passage in question is on p.371).

26. Badura-Skoda, *Bach-Interpretationen: Die Klavierwerke Johann Sebastian Bachs* (Laaber: Laaber, 1990), 217.

other hand, recalls in its thematic outline and character the famous G-minor aria of Pamina, "Ach, ich fühl's," in *The Magic Flute*, a piece similarly associated with despair and death; this Mozartian precedent may have influenced Beethoven's unusual choice of key at this advanced stage of the finale. As in *The Magic Flute*, the subjective despair of the lament is relieved seemingly through an outside agency. Only after an astonishing reinterpretation of the cadence of the lament in G major instead of G minor, marked by ten swelling chords, and movement through a kind of fugal labyrinth marked "nach u. nach sich neu belebend" ("gradually coming anew to life") does the continuation reach the tonic key of A♭ major, ultimately dispensing with the fugal texture in the closing passages of lyric euphoria.

We should consider here the implications of Beethoven's *Kunstvereingigung* in op. 110 and its narrative structure. According to Martin Cooper's interpretation of the fugal sections, "Beethoven's reply to the human grief and distress of the two arioso stanzas is the contemplation of a harmonious world whose laws are absolute and objective, neither subject to human passion nor concerned with anything beyond themselves."[27] Yet this judgment would seem to apply far more to the first fugue, which, as Cooper points out, is "almost immaculately traditional in form," than to the second, whose freedoms go well beyond Baroque models. Indeed, Beethoven's "nach u. nach sich neu belebend" and the related progression from *una corda* to *tutte le corde* with a slowing down in tempo—leading subsequently to a restoration of both the basic tempo and the tonic A♭ major when the fugal subject appears in octaves in the bass—imply that "contemplation of a harmonious world whose laws are absolute and objective" is insufficient to hold the balance against the despair of the arioso stanzas. Rather, the contrapuntal matrix of the second fugue, beginning in inversion and *una corda*, with its detached, remote quality, needs to be infused with a new energy, an energy that arises not naturally through traditional fugal procedures but only through an exertion of will that strains those processes to their limits and ends by overthrowing the self-contained texture of fugue altogether.

In this connection, Donald Francis Tovey stresses that in the closing fugue Beethoven eschewed an "organ-like climax" with its ascetic connotations as a "negation of the world": "Like all Beethoven's visions, this fugue absorbs

27. Martin Cooper, *Beethoven: The Last Decade, 1817–1827* (London: Oxford University Press, 1970), 194.

and transcends the world."[28] This open, comprehensive quality of op. 110 is conveyed through Beethoven's incorporation of the comic, scherzo-like second movement, with its use of two folk songs, as well as through his apparent allusion to that movement during the double diminution passage of the fugue, marked "Meno Allegro" (ex. 4a, b, and c).[29] The rhythmic and registral correspondence between these passages renders the beginning of the double-diminution passage transparent to the second folk-song quotation, "Ich bin lüderlich, du bist lüderlich," reinforcing Tovey's sense of an absorption of the "world"; the parallel is clearly audible, in part because Beethoven alters the fugal subject structurally at this point by deleting the second of the three rising fourths. Both motives stress the fourths spanning A♭ to E♭ and C to G, which are inverted in the fugue, and the placement of faster note values is parallel.

The rhythmic developments that point the way out of Beethoven's fugal labyrinth distort the subject, compressing it almost beyond recognition while simultaneously opening a means of connection to the earlier movements of the cycle through what Carl Dahlhaus calls "subthematic figuration."[30] In this sense, the Meno Allegro marks a crucial stage of emancipation from the apparent self-sufficiency of the fugue, with the rhythmic energy introduced through its double diminution becoming autonomous as it "bursts into flame," to quote Tovey.[31] What remains of the fugal texture after the return to A♭ major is a sequence of entries of the main subject in the bass, alto, and soprano in turn, followed by an extension based on the syncopated passage from the middle of the first fugue (mm. 40–46). The work concludes in lyric euphoria, capped by an expanded unfolding of the subject beginning in the higher register. After surmounting two diminished-seventh chords, the music finds its resolution in the arpeggiation of an emphatic and widely spaced A♭ major chord.

28. Donald Francis Tovey, *A Companion to Beethoven's Pianoforte Sonatas* (London: The Associated Board of the Royal Schools of Music, 1931), 270, 285–86. In this connection, see also Mellers, *Beethoven and the Voice of God*, 238–39.

29. See Cooper, *Beethoven: The Last Decade*, 190–91; A. B. Marx, *Ludwig van Beethoven: Leben und Schaffen* (1859; 5th ed. Berlin, 1901), vol. 2, 416.

30. See Dahlhaus, *Ludwig van Beethoven: Approaches to His Music*, trans. Mary Whittall (Oxford: Clarendon, 1991), 202–18.

31. Tovey, *Companion to Beethoven's Pianoforte Sonatas*, 270.

EX. 4. *a*, Popular song "Ich bin lüderlich, du bist lüderlich" (from Cooper, *Beethoven: The Last Decade*).
*b*, Piano Sonata, op. 110, Allegro molto.
*c*, Piano Sonata, op. 110, double diminution passage in fugue

The entire second fugue in op. 110 is thus subsumed into a larger transitional process whose symbolic assocations are identified in Beethoven's inscription "nach u. nach sich neu belebend." Here, as elsewhere in his later music, Beethoven does not employ fugue as an independent entity but merges it into an encompassing narrative design. The same tendency can be observed in other fugues of these years, which typically culminate in a climactic sonority after which the fugal texture is discontinued. The second section of the Credo fugue in the *Missa solemnis* peaks and is discontinued at the vast E♭ chord set to *saeculi*, whereas the analogous sonority in the penultimate "Diabelli" variation —also a two-part fugue—is the massive dissonant diminished-seventh chord over a pedal arpeggiated across the entire keyboard and which then serves as the transitional bridge to the final variation. Only within the circumscribed confines of a single earlier "Diabelli" variation—the sublime Fughetta, variation 24—does Beethoven allow himself to indulge in a rounded, lyrical fugal essay reminiscent of some of the organ pieces in Bach's *Clavierübung III*; but even here, dramatic contrast is supplied by the ensuing variation 25, with its comic reincarnation of Diabelli's commonplace waltz.

Two other "Diabelli" variations respond to the music of Bach, but neither is fugal. In variation 29, Beethoven writes a sort of Baroque lament on a very simple harmonic scheme, in which each measure of the first half alternates between tonic and dominant. Once again, a relation to the E♭-minor prelude from Book 1 of the Well-Tempered Clavier can be observed, a piece that in texture and sentiment is strikingly parallel to the Adagio ma non troppo in the Variations. This extensive reference to Bach seems fitting in light of the fact that the only variation cycle comparable to op.120, in scale and magnificence, is the "Goldberg" Variations.

The great Largo, variation 31, again shows the influence of Bach. Charles Rosen has characterized this variation as "an imitation of the ornamented minor variation of the *Goldberg*."[32] That Beethoven knew the "Goldberg" Variations has not been documented, but Diabelli's announcement of the publication of op.120 invokes the comparison: he proclaimed these Variations "a great and important masterpiece worthy to be ranked with the imperishable creations of the Classics," entitled "to a place beside Sebastian Bach's masterpiece in the same form." Melodic and textural similarities also imply Beethoven's acquaintance with Bach's "Goldberg" set, though of course the relationship suggests less an imitation than an homage to Bach. The beginning of each variation (Bach's variation 25 and Beethoven's variation 31), for example, is based on a melodic descending minor sixth (ex. 5a and b). At the end of each variation half, Beethoven's descending closing motive bears a striking resemblance to Bach's (ex. 6a and b). Moreover, Beethoven follows Bach in his florid texture within which important melody notes are stressed by an upward leap, usually of an octave. In the face of this evidence, it is difficult not to assume Beethoven's familiarity with the "Goldbergs." In the "Diabelli" Variations, the references to Bach and particularly to the "Goldberg" Variations also form part of a fascinating series of stylistic allusions to other composers—a directional sequence that culminates in Beethoven's self-reference, in the coda of

32. Rosen, *The Classical Style: Haydn, Mozart, Beethoven* (New York: Norton, 1972), 439.

EX. 5. *a*, Beethoven, "Diabelli" Variations, Var. 31, opening.
*b*, Bach, "Goldberg" Variations, Var. 25, opening

the final variation, to the finale from his last sonata, the variations on the Arietta of op. 111.[33]

Two of the monumental achievements of Beethoven's later years — the "Diabelli" Variations and the *Missa solemnis* — may represent on one level his conscious attempt to match the legacy of Bach, an endeavor reminiscent of Beethoven's earlier struggle during his first Vienna decade to establish his claim on the string quartet and symphony, genres then dominated by Haydn and Mozart. In the publisher's announcement of 1818 for the publication of Bach's B Minor Mass, Hans Georg Nägeli described that work as the "greatest musical work of art of all times and peoples." Soon after, by 1819, Beethoven began to compose his great Mass in D, the main labors on which continued until 1822, filling four large-formal sketchbooks and many pocket sketchbooks and loose leaves. Specific parallels between the *Missa solemnis* and B Minor Mass are hard to identify, and Handel's influence is sometimes more tangible. Still, the reputation of Bach's work may have helped shape Beethoven's attitude toward this magnum opus of his last decade. He was generally disinclined to describe any particular work as his greatest, but the *Missa solemnis* is an exception, a

33. For a more detailed discussion, see William Kinderman, *Beethoven's Diabelli Variations* (Oxford: Clarendon, 1987), esp. 111–30.

EX. 6. *a*, Beethoven, "Diabelli" Variations, Var. 31, bar 5a.
*b*, Bach, "Goldberg" Variations, Var. 25, bar 31

circumstance perhaps understandable as a response to Hans Georg Nägeli's well-publicized claim for Bach's Mass, as Marianne Helms has suggested.[34] On 5 June 1822, Beethoven wrote to the Leipzig publisher Carl Friedrich Peters, claiming that "the greatest work that I have so far composed is a large Mass with chorus and four solo voices and large orchestra," and to Schott in Mainz he reiterated the same claim: "So I indeed regard it as my greatest work."

\* \* \*

Discussions of Beethoven's late style have often invoked Bach's later music not only as a compositional influence but as a parallel situation. Dahlhaus claims that the concept of composers' "late works" stems essentially from the oeuvres of Bach, Beethoven, and Liszt: " 'Late works' do not belong, in terms of either cultural or musical history, to the eras in which chronology has placed them, yet they do not find spiritual homes in other eras. Bach's *Kunst der Fuge* and *Musikalisches Opfer* seem just as awkward and out of place in the age of *Emp-*

---

34. In her review of Maynard Solomon's *Beethoven*, in *Beethoven-Jahrbuch 1978/81*, 387. For information on Beethoven's great interest in Bach's Mass in B Minor but his lack of success in getting hold of it, see George B. Stauffer, *Bach: Mass in B Minor* (New York: Schirmer, 1997), 187–89.

*findsamkeit* as Beethoven's late string quartets in the Romantic era or Liszt's late piano works in the 'neo-Romantic.'"[35]

This quality of "homelessness," in Dahlhaus's view, signals an anticipatory modernity but not a progressive role in generating an immediate ongoing tradition. Noteworthy here is Adorno's argument that the aging Beethoven "sees through" the classical style as classicism, exposing its affirmative or festive aspects to a critique that puts into question that unity of subjectivity and objectivity that sustained his own earlier style.[36] An expansion of artistic range is furthered in part by the heightened contrasts and discontinuities of Beethoven's late style, and there may be at least a limited analogy here to Bach. An enhanced historical consciousness is characteristic of the later music of both composers. Robert Marshall, for instance, has drawn attention to modern elements in Bach's later music that rub shoulders with the conservative *stile antico*.[37] Thus a modern, sonorous Italianate style in the "Christe eleison" is juxtaposed with a stern *stile antico* in the second "Kyrie eleison" in the B-Minor Mass, while archaic styles in some late keyboard works, such as the vocal, ricercar-like E-Major Fugue in Book 2 of the Well-Tempered Clavier, coexist with an up-to-date, virtuoso keyboard figuration in the "Goldberg" Variations (suggesting Domenico Scarlatti's influence).

Beethoven's use of older styles included the assimilation of Gregorian and other conscious archaisms into several of the most ambitious pieces from the last decade of his life. The *Missa solemnis*, in particular, shows his indebtedness to sacred composition from the sixteenth and seventeenth centuries and his assimilation of the traditional rhetoric of Mass composition. The greatest his-

---

35. Dahlhaus, *Ludwig van Beethoven: Approaches to His Music*, 219.

36. Cf. Adorno's essay "Verfremdetes Hauptwerk. Zur Missa Solemnis," in his *Moments musicaux* (Frankfurt: Suhrkamp, 1964), 167–85, esp.183, and his article "Spätstil Beethovens" in the same volume. The German text of the passage cited reads as follows: "Er durchschaut die Klassik als Klassizismus. Er lehnt sich auf gegen das Affirmative, unkritisch das Sein Bejahende in der Idee der klassischen Symphonik; jenen Zug, den Georigiades in seiner Arbeit über das Finale der Jupiter-Symphonie festlich nannte." Also, see Adorno, *Beethoven: Philosophie der Musik: Fragmente und Texte: Fragment gebliebener Schriften*, vol.1, ed. Rolf Tiedemann (Frankfurt: Suhrkamp, 1993).

37. Marshall, "Bach the Progressive: Observations on His Later Works," *Musical Quarterly* 62 (1976): 313–57.

torical strokes in the Mass, however, rely not on assimilation of tradition but on the bold juxtaposition of different idioms. For his setting of the "Incarnatus est," Beethoven revived the Dorian mode, yet moments later, at the words "et homo factus est," the music shifts into D major, with the warmth of modern tonality. This passage derives power not only from the remote ethos of the distant past but from our sense that the later idiom is actually an advance, that the birth of tonality is itself capable of dramatizing the birth (or rebirth) of humankind. An equally startling throwback to earlier music in the Credo is the setting of "Et resurrexit tertia die secundum scripturas" as unaccompanied vocal polyphony in the Mixolydian mode.

In other archaizing passages in the Mass, and in the G-major section of the Ninth Symphony finale, there is often no sense that these historical references are superseded, as they are in the Credo of the Mass. In the Ninth Symphony, the archaism of expression surfacing at "Seid umschlungen Millionen" and at "Bruder, über'm Sternenzelt muss ein lieber Vater wohnen" is embodied in modal inflections as well as in the unison voices and trombones.[38] The awe-inspiring solemnity of such passages owes much to the archaic juxtaposition of adjacent triads, such as the lurch from a B♭ major chord at "Schöpfer" ("Creator") to the C-major sonority with "Welt?" ("world?") at "Ahnest du den Schöpfer, Welt?" ("Do you sense the Creator, world?") (ex. 7). Beethoven's anticipation of the shift to the C-major chord in the orchestra emphasizes the implied transcendental presence, while also opening the sonorous path to the ensuing dominant-seventh of D and therewith to the impressive deceptive shift to the monolithic climax on the high E♭ major chord at "Über Sternen muß er wohnen" — the registral ceiling and sublime endpoint of this collective gaze into the infinite.

While such passages rely vitally upon an assimilation of older musical techniques, their aesthetic significance seems more modernistic than antiquarian. This brings us back to Dahlhaus's apparently paradoxical point about "late style" as a modern and yet not immediately progressive phenomenon. The issue was addressed in different terms by Donald Francis Tovey: "The same spirit of truthfulness that makes Sebastian Bach hold himself aloof from the progressive art which he encourages in his sons, drives Beethoven to invent

---

38. Cf. Cooper, *Beethoven: The Last Decade 1817–1827*, 337–39.

EX.7. (*continued*)

107

new forms and new means of expression in every work he writes."[39] In other words, what sustains the late style of these composers is no passive response to current trends but a strong conviction about artistic synthesis—*Kunstvereinigung*, in Beethoven's phrase—whereby older forms assume new shapes. Here may lie the deepest roots of connection between what we have described as Beethoven's procedural or structural assimilation and his stylistic assimilation of Bach's music. In a broad sense, Beethoven's music combines the art of dramatic symmetries perfected by Haydn and Mozart with another, older tradition, whose *Festigkeit* was embodied above all in the works of Bach. On the one hand, this solidity was reflected in a growing contrapuntal density, culminating in Beethoven's claim as reported by Karl Holz of "a new type of voice-leading" ("eine neue Art der Stimmführung") in the last quartets.

At the same time, the quality of *Festigkeit* also had to do with a strength or consistency of musical character. Beethoven's highly integrated and even deterministic aesthetic stands in contrast to the art of colorful juxtaposition that was brought to its highest development by Mozart. The compelling force of the dramatic narrative continuity in Beethoven owes much to the older Baroque aesthetic of a unity of character; in this sense, his entire artistic enterprise rested on a synthesis of stylistic traditions that seemed to be independent of or even antagonistic to one another. The merging of Bachian solidity and continuity with the dramatic contrasts and discontinuities of the Classical style lends to Beethoven's art a unique richness and power. And in this context, his lifelong interest in Bach seems to have assumed an enabling role in the ongoing development of his style, sustaining his drive "to invent new forms and new means of expression," in Tovey's words. Since Beethoven, Bach's music has of course assumed an enabling role in the stylistic development of generations of composers. Chopin assimilated Bach's language into an aesthetic of pianistic brilliance and operatic lyricism; Wagner absorbed it into the ritualized diatonic polyphony of *Die Meistersinger* and *Parsifal*; Mahler's study of Bach lent weight to the third and fifth movements of the Fifth Symphony and to subsequent works as well. Yet there is no other composer for whom the influence of Bach was more important than for Beethoven.

---

39. Tovey, article on "J. S. Bach" in *The Encyclopaedia Britannica*, 11th ed. (London and New York: Encyclopaedia Britannica Company, 1910), vols. 3–4, p. 126.

# Bach, Brahms, and the Emergence of Musical Modernism

### Walter Frisch

In the spring of 1879, upon the death of Ernst Friedrich Richter, Johannes Brahms was offered the post of Thomaskantor at Leipzig. He was intrigued enough to make a few inquiries, especially among his friends the Herzogenbergs. But despite the possible attraction of stepping almost literally into the shoes of Johann Sebastian Bach, Brahms could not envision giving up his independence as a *freischaffender* composer. He declined, recommending instead Wilhelm Rust from Berlin.[1]

Taking Bach's old job would have represented only the most superficial gesture of homage or identification for someone whose involvement with the music of Bach—as editor, arranger, performer, conductor, collector, advisor, and, of course, as composer—was probably the most profound and extensive of any major figure of the nineteenth century.

The purpose of the following essay is not to survey Brahms's Bach reception, a task that has in any case been managed effectively, and from many different angles, by a number of scholars.[2] Instead, I wish to suggest that Brahms's

1. See Brahms's inquiries to the Herzogenbergs about the position, and their later remarks on Rust, in Johannes Brahms, *The Herzogenberg Correspondence*, ed. Max Kalbeck, trans. Hannah Bryant (New York: Da Capo, 1987), 83–85, 125.

2. The most comprehensive and fully documented study is still Siegmund Helms, "Johannes Brahms und Johann Sebastian Bach," *Bach-Jahrbuch* 57 (1971): 13–81. Other aspects of the Brahms-Bach relationship have been taken up by Daniel Beller-McKenna, "The Great *Warum?* Job, Christ, and Bach in a Brahms Motet," *Nineteenth-Century Music* 19 (1996): 231–51; David Brodbeck, "The Brahms-Joachim Counterpoint Exchange; or, Robert, Clara, and 'the Best Harmony between Jos. and Joh.,'" in *Brahms Studies*, vol.1, ed. David Brodbeck (Lincoln:

relationship to the music of Bach represented a special moment in Bach reception of the Romantic era. A generation or two later, especially in the works of Max Reger and other composers writing around 1900, a very different image of Bach became characteristic of, and perhaps a catalyst to, early musical modernism.

* * *

The aesthetics of Bach in nineteenth-century Germany and Austria can be said to have two main streams, which converge or mingle at many points. One stream, beginning at the very outset of the century, is dominated by the image of Bach as absolute musician. Known mainly for and through his keyboard works, especially the Well-Tempered Clavier and Art of Fugue, Bach was seen by early Romantics like Tieck, Wackenroder, and E. T. A. Hoffmann as an embodiment of pure instrumental music.[3] "The 'true' Bach of the nineteenth century," says Carl Dahlhaus, our most trenchant commentator on the metaphysics of autonomous instrumental music, "was the instrumental composer: a 'composer's composer' whose works were held up as paradigms of absolute music."[4] Needless to say this was also understood as a tradition of purely Ger-

---

University of Nebraska Press, 1994), 30–80; Carmen Debryn, "Kolorit und Struktur: Bachs Concerto 'O ewiges Feuer' (BWV 34) in Brahms' Bearbeitung," in *Beiträge zur Geschichte des Konzerts: Festschrift Siegfried Kross zum 60. Geburtstag*, ed. Reinmar Emans und Matthias Wendt (Bonn: Gudrun Schröder, 1990), 249–71; Imogen Fellinger, "Brahms und die Musik vergangener Epochen," in *Die Ausbreitung des Historismus über die Musik*, ed. Walter Wiora (Regensburg: Bosse, 1969), 147–63; Virginia Hancock, *Brahms's Choral Compositions and His Library of Early Music* (Ann Arbor: UMI Research Press, 1983), and Hancock, "Brahms's Performances of Early Choral Music," *Nineteenth-Century Music* 8 (1984): 125–41; William Horne, "Brahms's Düsseldorf Suite Study and His Intermezzo, Opus 116 No. 2," *Musical Quarterly* 73 (1989): 249–83; Siegfried Kross, *Die Chorwerke von Brahms*, 2d ed. (Berlin and Wunsiedl: Max Hesse, 1963); and Christoph Wolff, "Brahms, Wagner, and the Problem of Historicism in Nineteenth-Century Music: An Essay," in *Brahms Studies: Analytical and Historical Perspectives*, ed. George S. Bozarth (Oxford: Clarendon Press, 1990), 7–11.

3. A comprehensive summary of Bach reception in the early nineteenth century, especially in Austria (including a listing of printed editions of Bach's music), is included in Martin Zenck, *Die Bach-Rezeption des Späten Beethovens* (Stuttgart: Franz Steiner, 1986), 4–131.

4. Carl Dahlhaus, "Zur Entstehung der romantischen Bach-Deutung," in his *Klassische und Romantische Musikästhetik* (Laaber: Laaber, 1988), 125. Unless otherwise noted, all translations in this essay are my own.

man music; from the very beginning, reception of Bach's instrumental music is bound up with nationalistic sentiment.

The second principal stream of Bach reception involves his sacred music, and here the key date is, of course, the "rediscovery" of the St. Matthew Passion in 1829.[5] The image and reputation of Bach as Protestant church musician developed across the nineteenth century from that point and, as Friedrich Blume has suggested, loomed especially large after midcentury. Among the testimony adduced by Blume for this aspect of Bach reception are the cantata volumes of the *Gesamtausgabe* of the Bach-Gesellschaft, the attempts to restore Lutheran church music, the Bach biographies of C. H. Bitter and Philipp Spitta, and the aesthetic-philosophical musings of Wilhelm Dilthey.[6]

Bach as absolute musician, as German, as Lutheran composer: all these images are refracted onto Brahms's reception. It might even be said that, in an instance of ontogeny recapitulating phylogeny, Brahms's early career reflects the nineteenth-century evolution of Bach reception. He began in the early 1850s as a composer of "absolute" or abstract keyboard works. Then, beginning in the later 1850s, he turned his attention to vocal works that, while not liturgical, are clearly imbued with Protestant religious spirit: the high points are the motets of opp. 29 and 74; the German Requiem, op. 45; and the *Triumphlied*, op. 55.[7]

\* \* \*

Many composers begin their careers modeling their works after those of time-honored masters. Brahms seems to have taken a somewhat different route. By the middle of 1854 Schumann's "young eagle," then only twenty-one, had already published boldly original works, including three piano sonatas (opp. 1,

5. See especially Martin Geck, *Die Wiederentdeckung der Matthäuspassion im 19. Jahrhundert* (Regensburg: Bosse, 1967).

6. Friedrich Blume, *Two Centuries of Bach* (New York: Da Capo, 1978), 58–70. Dilthey's essay on Bach forms part of his larger chapter or section, "Die Grosse Deutsche Musik des 18. Jahrhunderts," in the posthumously issued book, Wilhelm Dilthey, *Von Deutscher Dichtung und Musik*, 2d ed. (Stuttgart: B. G. Teubner, 1957), 205–48.

7. A book in progress by Daniel Beller-McKenna, tentatively entitled *Nationalism in the Sacred Music of Johannes Brahms*, will explore more fully the ideological and political context of Brahms's sacred vocal music (and his Bach reception). I am grateful to Prof. Beller-McKenna for sharing his book proposal with me.

2, 5), a scherzo (op. 4) and a set of variations also for piano (op. 9), some Lieder (opp. 3, 6, 7), and an expansive piano trio (op. 8). Although this series of works clearly owes something to Beethoven, Schubert, Schumann, and Chopin, the music is anything but epigonic.[8]

Brahms's was then an impressive start for any composer. But he was not satisfied. By late 1854 he stopped composing larger works and entered into a kind of self-imposed study period in which the music of Bach played a critical role. Among the fruits of the years 1854–55 are a group of dance movements for piano, catalogued as WoO 3–5 in the Brahms *Werkverzeichnis:*

woo 3: Two Gavottes, A minor and A major
woo 4: Two Gigues, A minor and B minor
woo 5: Two Sarabandes, A minor and B minor

These movements appear to have been intended as part of complete keyboard suites modeled directly on the those of Bach.[9] If he had not encountered them in his Hamburg period, Brahms would have studied the French and English Suites and the Partitas in the library of Robert Schumann, in whose house he was living, after the elder composer had been moved to the asylum in Endenich.

An examination of Brahms's Sarabande in A Minor (ex. 1a), which he was later to rework for the middle movement of his Quintet, op. 88, shows how impressively Brahms absorbed elements of the Bach style into his own developing romantic idiom. Undoubtedly sources of inspiration for this piece can be found among many different movements of Bach's dance suites, but I think the closest model in many respects is the Sarabande of the Third English Suite in G minor (ex. 2a). Some of the similarities are quite striking:

– Like the Bach, the Brahms unfolds over a tonic pedal for six (in Bach, seven) of the eight measures of the first half.

8. On the piano sonatas and the trio, see my *Brahms and the Principle of Developing Variation* (Berkeley and Los Angeles: University of California Press, 1984), chap. 2. On the scherzo, see my essay, "Brahms: From Classical to Modern," in *Nineteenth-Century Piano Music*, ed. R. Larry Todd (New York: Schirmer Books, 1990), 318–20. On the variations, see Oliver Neighbour, "Brahms and Schumann: Two Opus Nines and Beyond," *Nineteenth-Century Music* 8 (1984): 266–70.

9. Robert Pascall, "Unknown Gavottes by Brahms," *Music and Letters* 57 (1976): 404–11; Horne, "Brahms's Düsseldorf Suite Study."

EX.1. *a*, Brahms, Sarabande, WoO 5, no.1 (prob. 1854).
*b*, Recomposition of mm. 9–13

EX.2. *a*, Bach, Sarabande from English Suite No.3 (BWV 808).
*b*, Bach, "les agréments" for mm.9–10

114

EX. 2. (*continued*)

- Both pieces begin with a characteristic, and motivically significant, downward eighth-note figure moving to a sustained note on the second beat. (The stressed second beat is a characteristic of the sarabande as a genre, of course.)
- In the first measure of both Bach and Brahms, the tenor voice moves up (in contrary motion to the upper part) by a half-step from the fifth degree to the minor sixth.
- At the opening of the second half of both pieces, the melodic eighth-note figure is inverted and leads to a higher register. The flourish or roulade that Brahms places on the third beat in mm. 9–10 seems very like the "agrément" that Bach places on his third beat of m. 9 in the decorated version of the Sarabande (ex. 2b).
- Both pieces settle in the key of VI (F major in Brahms, m. 12; E-flat in Bach, m. 16) in the middle of their second sections, before the return to the tonic. This is an unusual tonal goal in Bach's small binary forms in the minor key; Brahms clearly noticed and admired Bach's strategy. (In the Bach, the E-flat arises as the relative major of the C minor reached in m. 12.)

Despite the many points of contact, Brahms's little Sarabande is far from a mere imitation of Bach's. The triplet rhythms, with their implication of 3 against 2, the delicate modal shifts, and the fluctuation between A major and minor—these Brahmsian features penetrate the Bach veneer.

Brahms writes his Sarabande more clearly in a rounded binary form; the return, actually to the second phrase, comes at m. 13 (cf. m. 5). In Bach the return is more disguised; when a melodic gesture resembling the opening arrives at m. 17, just after the VI chord, he is still far away from the tonic, which is in fact reached only in the very last measure.

The way in which Brahms approaches his tonic is less complex, but nonetheless very elegant. After m. 10, Brahms abandons the sequence at the opening of the second half in order to lead toward F major, which is reached on

115

the last beat of m. 12 (without its fifth). This chord, wonderfully ambiguous in its context, moves directly to the A minor that begins the return. Brahms has managed to arrive at the tonic directly from the sixth degree, bypassing the dominant altogether. It is a strategy he would use again many times in his instrumental works.

A lesser composer might have opted for a more conventional return at this point, as in example 1b, where I have recomposed the passage to continue the sequence for one more measure, leading directly to the dominant in m. 12. This mundane, much cruder version simply composes out across four measures the A–G–F–E motion in the bass. Brahms's solution, which makes F the goal and avoids the E, is infinitely more sophisticated and suggestive.

Almost forty years after completing this piece, when asked one day by his friend Theodor Billroth to describe the signs of "beauty" in a melody, Brahms adduced the sarabandes of the French Suites as models. Billroth reported Brahms's thoughts in a passage that merits citation because it counts as Brahms's most extended surviving reflection on Bach:

Vienna, 19 November 1893

Sunday morning at Brahms's place. I wanted to hear from him something about the shaping of melody, about marks of "beauty" in a melody. [There follows an account of Brahms's analysis of Goethe's poem "Über allen Gipfeln."] For a similar analysis Brahms used some sarabandes from the French Suites of Bach. The articulation of the whole, the ascent of the melody. Question and answer. The endings of the individual periods (cadences). The contrary motion of the upper voice and the bass to and from one another: the principal means for a beautiful effect—[for] the harmonic. The half cadences and bold turns of the cadence to a dissonance that leads to a distant key. The melodic-harmonic surprise, the skillful transposition of chords to soften a dissonance. The skillful return to the original key, gentler and harsher sounds, their connections. Longer final cadences. — In the second parts: insertion of longer cadences, longer lingering in the more distant keys. Beautiful preparations of the return to the original key.

Now the leading of the middle voices, their groupings and relation to bass and soprano. (In contrast to this: empty, ugly, clumsy melodies, distorted motions, poor-sounding or empty basses.)

In the repetitions, changes that with good composers are always intensifications and improvements.

In the doubles, "veiling" of the melody.
*"The more an artwork is chewed up, the tastier it will be."* [10]

These analytical comments about phrase structure, harmonic motion and modulation, counterpoint, voice-leading, and formal processes all reflect basic musical values, stemming largely from Bach, that were held by Brahms throughout his life. I would argue that the Bach sarabandes taught Brahms principles that he applied not only in the smaller dimensions of his early dance pieces, his waltzes (the op.39 and *Liebeslieder* sets, opp.52 and 65), and his late piano pieces, but also on the much larger scale of the sonata form. Many of the retransitions in his first movements, for example, show the same "beautiful preparations of the return to the original key" that he admired in Bach and also displayed in his own early Sarabande.

In 1892, just a year before making his remarks on the French Suites, Brahms displayed in the Intermezzo op.116, no.2 how large a role the tradition of the Bach sarabande continued to play for him (ex.3). As William Horne has suggested, there is in the Intermezzo "an astonishingly close affinity" to Brahms's

10. Sonntag vormittag bei Brahms. Ich wollte von ihm etwas über Melodienbildung hören, über Zeichen der "Schönheit" einer Melodie. . . . Zu einer ähnlichen Analyse verwendete Brahms einige S a r a b a n d e n a u s d e n f r a n z ö s i c h e n S u i t e n von Bach. Die Gliederung des Ganzen, das Aufsteigen der Melodie. Frage und Antwort. Die Schlüsse der einzelnen Perioden (Kadenzen). Die Gegenbewegung der Oberstimme und des Basses zu- und voneinander: Hauptmoment für die schöne Wirkung—das Harmonische. Die Halbschlüsse und kühnen Wendungen der Kadenz zu einer Dissonanz, die in eine fernliegende Tonart führt. Die melodisch-harmonische Überraschung, die geschickte Umlagerung der Akkorde, um eine Dissonanz abzuschwächen. Das geschickte Zurückgehen in die ursprüngliche Tonart, weichere und herbere Klänge, ihre Verbindungen. Längere Schlußkadenzen. — In den zweiten Teilen: Einschiebungen längerer Kadenzen, längeres Verbleiben in den entfernteren Tonarten. Schöne Vorbereitungen zur Rückkehr in die ursprüngliche Tonart.

Nun die Führung der Mittelstimmen, ihre Gruppierungen und Verhalten zu Baß und Sopran. (Im Gegensatze hiezu: Leere, häßliche, ungeschickte Melodien, verdrehte Bewegungen. Schlechtklingende oder leere Bässe.)

Bei den Wiederholungen Veränderungen, die bei guten Komponisten immer Steigerungen und Verschönerungen sind.

Bei den Doubles "Verschleierungen" der Melodie.

"Je m e h r e i n K u n s t w e r k v e r k a u t, u m s o s c h m a c k h a f t e r w i r d e s." *Billroth und Brahms im Briefwechsel*, ed. Otto Gottlieb-Billroth (Berlin and Vienna: Urban & Schwarzenberg, 1935), 475–76; cited in Helms, "Brahms und Bach," 46.

EX. 3. Brahms, Intermezzo, op. 116, no. 2 (1892)

early sarabandes.[11] The Intermezzo is in triple meter, begins on the downbeat
with an eighth-note figure that leads to a sustained second beat, exploits the
two-against-three rhythms, now explicitly between the hands, and consists of
four-measure phrases (with an extra "cadential reiteration," as Horne calls it).
The diminished-seventh chord over the tonic pedal in m. 2 of the Intermezzo
is precisely the same chord as in mm. 1–2 of the earlier Sarabande.

As in the Sarabande, there is a fluctuation between minor and major, involving both the tonic and the subdominant, and now it is even more sophisticated.
In m. 5, the first measure of the second phrase or consequent, the two forms of
the tonic are juxtaposed in a single measure: the A-minor chord of beat 1 moves
to A major in beat 2. This is less a change of mode, however, than it is a harmonic move from the tonic minor to the dominant of IV; the ambiguity is fully
characteristic of Brahms. The next measure repeats but transforms the process

11. Horne, "Brahms's Düsseldorf Suite Study," 270. There is no documentary evidence to support Horne's claim that this Intermezzo may have originated in the 1850s and been intended
for one of the early suites. Brahms's biographer Max Kalbeck asserts, as so often without any
direct evidence, that some of the piano pieces of op. 116 were written earlier than 1892, possibly
as early as the Düsseldorf period (*Johannes Brahms* [Berlin: Deutsche Brahms-Gesellschaft,
1904–14], 4:277).

on the subdominant: D minor moves not to D major, but to a diminished-seventh chord on D♯ that has the major third of D, F♯, within it.

With this Intermezzo, any Bach influence may be said to be completely absorbed into Brahms's mature style. Although he was no longer poring over it in Schumann's study, no longer performing it in public, and no longer actively teaching it to students like Eugenie Schumann and Florence May, Brahms obviously retained a passionate involvement with Bach's keyboard music to the end of his life.

* * *

I do not interpret either the Sarabande or the Intermezzo as a case of Bloomian "misreading" of the kind that some commentators, notably Kevin Korsyn, have detected in works by Brahms, including the Quintet movement based on the Sarabande.[12] To my ear, there is little evidence for a kind of agonistic struggle with a powerful precursor that characterizes the "anxiety of influence." Indeed, I think it would be difficult to posit this kind of a model for the relationship of any of Brahms's works to those of Bach. The Bloom scenario may work better for Brahms's relationship with Beethoven, as manifested in works like Brahms's First Piano Concerto and First Symphony.[13] Beethoven, closer to Brahms in chronological time and in compositional tradition, is in this sense more of a threatening father figure than Bach.

A more useful path for understanding, or at least probing, the Brahms-Bach relationship is opened up by the concept of historicism. This is a term with an almost infinite variety of nuances and usages. In its most general meaning historicism, or *Historismus* in German, indicates an awareness and knowledge of, and usually respect for, the past, as well as an attempt to incorporate it into one's artistic language. In its most blatant form the historicist impulse can lead to eclecticism or pastiche; an egregious example from the music of the

12. Kevin Korsyn, "Toward a New Poetics of Musical Influence," *Music Analysis* 10 (1991): 3–72. See Richard Taruskin's fine discussion of this article, and of the problems involved in applying Bloom's theories to music, in "Revising Revision," *Journal of the American Musicological Society* 46 (1993): 114–38.

13. For a persuasive Bloom-inspired reading of this aspect of the finale of Brahms's First Symphony, see Reinhold Brinkmann, *Late Idyll: The Second Symphony of Johannes Brahms*, trans. Peter Palmer (Cambridge, Mass.: Harvard University Press, 1995), 44–53.

earlier nineteenth century is Louis Spohr's "Historical Symphony" of 1839, in which each movement is written in a different style ranging from Bach to the (then) present.[14] A somewhat analogous phenomenon in architecture is Vienna's Ringstrasse of the 1870s, in which each monumental building was created in an individual historical style.[15] At the opposite end of the spectrum are works like Brahms's little Intermezzo, or perhaps the finale of his Fourth Symphony, where historicism really becomes indistinguishable from a composer's or artist's own style.

Historicism implies, but is not identical to, historical awareness or situatedness. Adorno claimed that music was "historical through and through," that history is a defining aspect of music's identity.[16] Many commentators, ranging from Dilthey and Gadamer to, within the profession of musicology, Dahlhaus and Treitler, have sought to reinforce that not only for creators, but also for listeners, viewers, and scholars, historicity—being "historical"—is a fundamental condition.[17]

Historicism is slightly different, an attitude or a stance rather than an inescapable given. For Dahlhaus, historicism implies "a conviction or feeling that past things form an essential part of the present precisely in being from the past, and not because of some substance within them that has withstood all change."[18] In this view historicism is not conservatism; it seeks not to resist

14. See Eric Doflein, "Historismus in der Musik," in *Die Ausbreitung des Historismus über die Musik*, ed. Walter Wiora (Regensburg: Bosse, 1969), 24–27; Walter Wiora, "Grenzen und Stadien des Historismus in der Musik," in *Die Ausbreitung*, 301; Siegfried Oechsle, *Symphonik nach Beethoven* (Kassel: Bärenreiter, 1992), 1–6.

15. See Carl Schorske, *Fin-de-Siècle Vienna* (New York: Knopf, 1980), chap. 2.

16. Cited in Carl Dahlhaus, *Foundations of Music History*, trans. J. Bradford Robinson (Cambridge: Cambridge University Press, 1983), 61.

17. For a useful survey of traditions and ideologies of history-writing in Germany, with much discussion of the meanings of "historicism," see Georg Iggers, *The German Conception of History*, rev. ed. (Wesleyan, Conn.: Wesleyan University Press, 1983). Dahlhaus's magisterial views are contained in his *Foundations*, especially the chapter "Historicism and Tradition," 53–71. Leo Treitler's statements and explorations are collected in his *Music and the Historical Imagination* (Cambridge, Mass.: Harvard University Press, 1989).

18. Dahlhaus, *Foundations*, 70; see also Dahlhaus, *Nineteenth-Century Music*, trans. J. Bradford Robinson (Berkeley and Los Angeles: University of California Press, 1989), 320–28.

change, but to acknowledge and even embrace it. For the historicist, "past and present form an indissoluble alloy."[19]

Within this conceptual framework, Brahms emerges as the great historicist among nineteenth-century composers, and his reception of Bach stands as perhaps the finest example of the "indissoluble alloy" kind of historicism. With very rare exceptions, Brahms did not wear Bach on his sleeve or seek to exaggerate the distance between himself and Bach. He was not prone to write fugues on B–A–C–H, like Schumann and Liszt—he preferred to encode the names of Clara or Robert Schumann into his compositions—or to end instrumental compositions with stirring chorales, like Mendelssohn.

\* \* \*

Brahms's historicism, as manifested in his Bach reception, is not especially anxious or troubled. But that he may have been the last major composer within the Austro-German tradition for whom this was true is suggested by a comparison of chorale preludes for organ by Brahms and Max Reger, a composer born in 1874, and thus almost two generations Brahms's junior.

Brahms's prelude based on the Passion chorale, "O Traurigkeit, o Herzeleid" (WoO 7), was composed in the 1850s, then published in slightly revised form in 1882, together with a fugue on the same chorale, as a supplement to an issue of the *Musikalisches Wochenblatt* in Leipzig (ex. 4 gives the revised version). This work is less well known, but no less beautiful, than the group of Eleven Chorale Preludes for Organ, op. 122, that Brahms composed in the spring of 1896 and that were to be his final works.

In "O Traurigkeit," as in the later set, op. 122, the models are the chorale preludes of Bach's *Orgelbüchlein*, those "symphonic poems in miniature" (as Reger called them), in which the chorale melody is normally present in the top line.[20] As in the A-minor Sarabande, Brahms's own style comes through quite clearly,

19. Dahlhaus, *Foundations*, 70.

20. There is no complete setting of the "O Traurigkeit" chorale in Bach's *Orgelbüchlein*, only a two-measure fragment in the key of F minor, which was published in the Bach Gesellschaft edition and which Brahms would likely have known. See Johann Sebastian Bach, *Organ Music* (New York: Dover, 1970), 206. An excellent recent study of the nineteenth-century reception of the *Orgelbüchlein* is Russell Stinson, *Bach: The Orgelbüchlein* (New York: Schirmer Books, 1996), chap. 7.

EX. 4. Brahms, Chorale Prelude on "O Traurigkeit, o Herzeleid," WoO 7 (comp. by 1858; revision pub. 1882), mm. 1–6

especially in the two-against-three rhythms, the subtle juxtaposition of major and minor, especially in mm. 1–2, and the splendid path that this juxtaposition allows Brahms to follow from the tonic of m. 1 to the dominant of m. 3. Also Brahmsian is the way in which, after the densest chromaticism of the prelude, at the climax in mm. 9–11, the harmonic air is suddenly cleared by the A-minor $^6_4$ chord that initiates the "recapitulation" in m. 12 (not shown in the example).

There would be many ways to "chew up" this piece analytically. But its achievement is perhaps best captured in the words of Brahms's friend Spitta. In 1873, not long after Spitta had sent Brahms the first volume of his Bach biography, the composer replied with a kind of thank-you note, a manuscript of a fugue based on "O Traurigkeit." Spitta replied: "In artistry and depth of feeling, in intimacy, I find it fully worthy of the models of the great Sebastian Bach, from which, however, it is distinguished by a certain subjective refinement, as occasioned by the present situation of music and the tendency of our time. I'm thereby implying that this organ piece seems to me in no way a mere copy [*bloße Nachahmung*], but an independent modeling [*selbständige Nachbildung*], which would be only to be expected from you."[21] These comments would certainly apply to the prelude as well.

In 1893, almost forty years after Brahms had composed the "O Traurigkeit" prelude, and about a decade after it was published in the *Musikalisches Wochenblatt*, the young Max Reger wrote a prelude for organ based on the same chorale, in the same key. It was published without opus number a year later, in 1894, in the *Allgemeine Musik-Zeitung*. At the time of composition, Reger was only nineteen, thus a few years younger — but in the same phase of early maturity — as Brahms had been when writing the Sarabande and "O Traurigkeit" prelude. The first half of Reger's work is given as example 5; the chorale melody is in the upper of the two pedal parts.[22]

This prelude is just one drop in the vast ocean of Reger's Bach-related musical activity, which encompassed not only many original works for organ, piano, and orchestra, but also hundreds of transcriptions, arrangements, and editions of Bach's music. There seems little question that quantitatively Reger had the greatest involvement with Bach of any composer since Bach himself.[23]

From this prelude we can detect a very different kind of Bach reception from that of Brahms, and a much more modern one, in many senses of that word. In Reger the chorale is overwhelmed by a tangle of polyphonic voices that seem

21. *Johannes Brahms Briefwechsel*, vol. 16 (Berlin: Deutsche-Brahms Gesellschaft, 1920/22), 51.

22. As several organists have pointed out to me, Reger may have been inspired by Bach's use of the double pedal in the chorale prelude *Aus tiefer Noth*, from *Clavierübung III*.

23. See the excellent study by Johannes Lorenzen, *Max Reger als Bearbeiter Bachs* (Wiesbaden: Breitkopf & Härtel, 1982). See also Friedhelm Krummacher, "Auseinandersetzung im Abstand: Über Regers Verhältnis zu Bach," in *Reger-Studien 5*, ed. Susanne Shigihara (Wiesbaden: Breitkopf & Härtel, 1993), 11–39; and Ludwig Finscher's essay in the present volume.

EX.5. Max Reger, Chorale Prelude on "O Traurigkeit, o Herzeleid,"
without opus number (1893)

125

to have grown out of control, like the tendrils of some aggressive vine. This prelude is inspired by the vision of Bach the Polyphonist that would feed into the twentieth-century concepts of the polyphonic "Bach culture" described by August Halm in 1913, and of "linear counterpoint," the term coined by Ernst Kurth in 1917 to characterize Bach's melodic style.[24]

What we have in Reger's prelude, I would suggest, is a genuinely anxious attitude toward Bach. There is a sense of a loss the composer is seeking to recover, or a distance he is trying to bridge, by overdetermining the counterpoint. Here we might return to Dahlhaus, who makes a distinction between two different kinds of historicism, "tradition" and "restoration." For Dahlhaus, tradition implies an unbroken and often unquestioning continuity with the past, while restoration implies the acknowledgement of a gulf, a gap, that must be bridged in an act of historicist understanding.[25]

Reger's is an almost desperate act of restoration, while in the Brahms—at least to my ear—there is much more of a sense of tradition, although it is never unquestioning. In these ways Brahms's historicism, and perhaps especially his Bach reception, differ radically from that of the generation that followed him. If Brahms's prelude reflects, as Spitta implied, a "certain subjective refinement" that somehow captured the "present situation of music and the tendency of our time" in 1873, Reger's seems to capture a very different situation and tendency two decades later.

\* \* \*

Something of this newer context is reflected by a survey or *Rundfrage* conducted in 1905 by the editors of the journal *Die Musik* in Berlin. They invited over two hundred composers, performers, scholars, critics, writers, and even poets to respond to the question "What does Johann Sebastian Bach mean to me and what is his importance for our time?" ("Was ist mir Johann Sebastian Bach und was bedeutet er für unsere Zeit?"). Apparently no major living figure in music was omitted in the survey. The editors did not restrict themselves to German-speaking lands: Mahler, Nikisch, and Guido Adler were

24. See August Halm, *Von Zwei Kulturen der Musik*, 3d ed. (Stuttgart: Klett, 1947; orig.1913); Ernst Kurth, *Die Grundlagen des linearen Kontrapunkts* (Bern: Drechsel, 1917).

25. Dahlhaus, *Foundations*, 67.

among those approached, but also Sibelius, Glazunov, Debussy, Puccini, Grieg, MacDowell, and Elgar.

The very idea of taking such a poll and then devoting seventy-five pages to reporting the results reveals a kind of radical historicism, one that acknowledges the loss, or at least the slipping away, of a tradition. This much seems to be acknowledged by the editors, who note: "The stimulus for our survey came from our readers. From numerous communications we have formed the impression that the 'Bach of Bachs' still represents a 'problem' today, whose solution many a mind is assiduously working to find."[26] The editors go on to say that all the historical, editorial, and philological work on Bach—and here they must mean the Bach Gesellschaft edition, completed in 1900, as well as the monumental biography of Spitta—has not pointed the way to the "Castalian source" from which Bach's "god-filled" soul sprang. The search for origins is a telltale sign of historicist thinking.

Approximately half of those people contacted responded, with comments ranging from a few phrases to a substantial essay. One is struck that among the responses, the idea of Bach as healer—as healing fountain or physician—in sick, troubled, or "hypernervous" times comes up repeatedly, often with specific medical terminology. Table 1 gives a sampling of these remarks.

For Max Reger, Bach was "a never-failing medicine or drug" (*nie versiegende Heilmittel*) that would be good not only for musicians but for everyone who "suffers from spinal problems of any kind" (*die an Rückenmarksschwindsucht jeder Art leiden*).[27] Reger referred to his age as *erkrankt*, diseased, from "misunderstood Wagner," and in need of such a cure. For Theodor Müller-Reuter, Bach is "a restorative spring into which I step when my musical soul has suffered some kind of damage. . . . Bach is like a physician to me."

The image of Bach as healer was in fact nothing new in the nineteenth century. The Bachian counterpoint in Beethoven's last sonatas and quartets—and let us even throw in here the more Palestrinian "Heiliger Dankgesang" from

---

26. "Was ist mir Johann Sebastian Bach und was bedeutet er für unsere Zeit?" *Die Musik* 5/1 (1905): 3.

27. Reger's response to the survey taken in 1905 by the journal *Die Musik:* "Was ist mir Johann Sebastian Bach und was bedeutet er für unsere Zeit?" *Die Musik* 5/1 (1905): 74. Also cited in Lorenzen, *Max Reger*, 53. *Rückenmarksschwindsucht* refers literally to loss of spinal fluid.

Table 1 *Sample of Responses to Rundfrage from Die Musik 5/1 (October 1905): 3–78*
*"Was ist mir Johann Sebastian Bach und was bedeutet er für unsere Zeit?"*
(arranged in order of composers' ages, from oldest to youngest)

FELIX DRAESEKE: "Bach ist gesund und natürlich, unsere gegenwärtige Zeit ungesund und unnatürlich." (p.12)

ALEXANDRE GUILMANT: "La musique de Bach est reposante, satisfait le coeur et l'esprit; elle le rend meilleur!" (p.13)

ALEXIS HOLLAENDER: "Für die Musik der Gegenwart bedeutet oder vielmehr sollte Bachs Musik ein Heilbad bedeuten, in dem sie sich aus dem Sport der sich überbietenden Sensationen reinigen, stärken und auf sich selber besinnen könnte." (pp.18–19)

FRITZ STEINBACH: "Was Sebastian Bach für unsere Zeit bedeutet? . . . frische Gesundheit in unserer Zeit drohender Verweichlichung . . ." (p.39)

THEODOR MÜLLER-REUTER: "Bach ist mir ein Gesundbrunnen, in den ich steige, wenn meine musikalische Seele irgend Schaden erlitten hat, ein Gesundbrunnen von stärkender und reinigender Wirkung, Kräfte des Widerstands gegen alle seichte, hypernervöse und ungesunde Musik gebend. — Bach ist mir ein Artzt, der durch seine Werke väterlich warnend zu mir spricht, der mir das Gewissen schärft und der mich heilt, wenn musikalische Exzesse die Gesundheit der Phantasie und Kunstübung gefährdet haben." (p.46)

FRANK VAN DER STUCKEN: "Für unsere neurasthenische Generation ist Bachs kerngesunde Kunst die segenbringende Nahrung der Musiker. . . . Ein gutes Heilmittel gegen Über- oder Unterschätzung eines Komponisten ist das Studium Bachscher Musik." (p.47)

WILHELM BERGER: "Bach ist der Urquell alles Gesunden in der Musik." (p.61)

LUDWIG THUILLE: "Wer den Geist Bachscher Musik voll zu erfassen imstande ist, der hat sich einen Gesundbrunnen gewonnen, den er zeitlebens nicht auszuschöpfen vermag." (p.62)

WALDEMAR VON BAUSSNERN: "Ohne Bach gibt es für uns keine Gesundheit . . ." (p.70)

MAX SCHILLINGS: "In unserem 'reizsamen' Zeitalter sollte keiner unterlassen, aus dem Gesundbrunnen Bach zu trinken, der der Stärkung für Herz und Hirn bedarf." (p.71)

MAX REGER: "Ein gar kräftigliches, nie versiegendes Heilmittel nicht nur für alle jene Komponisten und Musiker, die an 'missverstandenem Wagner' erkrankt sind, sondern für alle jene 'Zeitgenossen,' die an Rückenmarksschwindsucht jeder Art leiden." (p.74)

the A-minor Quartet op. 132 — clearly suggests a restorative, a cure. In the summer and fall of 1845 Robert Schumann, suffering from a bad bout of mental illness, turned to an intensive study of counterpoint, and especially Bach's music, which seems to have had a therapeutic effect.[28] The mortally ill Brahms also found Bach comforting. His biographer Max Kalbeck reported, concerning his last visit with Brahms in March 1897: "He [Brahms] complained about his situation and said: 'It's lasting so long.' He also told me that he was not able to listen to any music. The piano remained closed; he could only read Bach, that was all. He pointed to the piano, where on the music stand, which stood on top of the closed cover, lay a score of Bach."[29]

One could probably multiply such examples from other nineteenth-century composers. Yet there is, I think, a difference between the highly personal view of Bach as healer revealed in these earlier cases and the broader social implications of the remarks cited from the 1905 survey in *Die Musik*. In 1905 most of the figures quoted were presumably in good health; for them, Bach is a balm for a culture that is seen as degenerate, perverted, effeminate, and unhealthy. *Degeneration* (*Entartung*) was, of course, the title of Max Nordau's notorious best-seller of 1893 on this topic; in its wake came many tracts diagnosing different aspects of modern culture and society.[30] Might Reger's "O Traurigkeit" prelude of the same year, 1893, be read as a statement on degeneration in musical culture, with an extra-heavy dose of Bachian polyphony proposed as cure? (Or is the piece rather, as conservative critics would have argued, a symptom of that degeneration?)

The Bach number of *Die Musik* was followed within two months, in December 1905, by the premiere of Strauss's *Salome*, the great *succès de scandale* of German modernism. The temporal proximity to the Bach survey is telling. The responses to that survey cited in table 1 are, if not the first reactions, then major catalytic elements, in the explosive debate about degeneracy in Austro-

28. See Peter Ostwald, *Schumann: The Inner Voices of a Musical Genius* (Boston: Northeastern University Press, 1985), 200. In August 1845 Schumann composed several fugues based on B-A-C-H for the organ or pedal piano (op. 60). Around this time he also wrote the Studies and Sketches for the pedal piano (opp. 56 and 58 respectively).

29. Cited in Helms, "Brahms und Bach," 13.

30. See the useful anthology of essays about the concept of "degeneration" in various aspects of culture and science in the later nineteenth century, *Degeneration: The Dark Side of Progress*, ed. J. Edward Chamberlin and Sander L. Gilman (New York: Columbia University Press, 1985).

German music. This much is acknowledged by Suzanne Shigihara, who has called the *Rundfrage* comments a "preliminary skirmish" (*Vorgeplankel*) in a dispute over musical and cultural values that would stretch over a decade to the beginning of World War I and would include polemical statements in musical journals and newspapers by Reger, Felix Draeseke, Hugo Riemann, and Richard Strauss, among others.[31]

Even Albert Schweitzer put in his two pfennig. In the German edition of his Bach study, published in 1908, Schweitzer added at the very end the plea that "Bach help our age to attain the spiritual unity and fervour of which it so sorely stands in need."[32] This sentence does not appear in the original French edition of 1905.

The crusty old Riemann, who entered the fray in 1908, saw the only hope for modern music in the study of earlier composers, including Bach. And here he took Brahms as the paradigm for how to assimilate the past. Composers should not seek to imitate Brahms's style, Riemann says: "Rather, following Brahms's path of a thorough study of the past is in fact the way that will lead us out of the present-day confusion of aesthetic ideas. The works of the past must be retrieved not only for their intrinsic worth, but for the healing of our decadent and degenerate creations, and also for the regeneration of our entire musical sensibility."[33]

That Riemann takes Brahms as a model shows how far musical culture had changed in the decade since the composer's death in 1897. In one sense, Riemann's position puts Bach and Brahms firmly into the same category: they become, in Dahlhaus's definition of historicism, "one indissoluble alloy." I would argue that this alloy—or at least the perception of it—dissolves with the arrival of modernism.

The case could also be made that the arguments of Reger, Riemann, and the respondents to the *Die Musik* survey constitute some of the first mani-

31. See Susanne Shigihara, ed., *"Die Konfusion in der Musik": Felix Draesekes Kampfschrift von 1906 und ihre Folgen* (Bonn: Gudrun Schröder, 1990), 1. This valuable anthology includes many of the polemical articles in this debate.

32. Albert Schweitzer, *J. S. Bach*, trans. [from the German ed.] Ernest Newman (Boston: Humphries, 1911; orig. French ed. 1905), 2:468.

33. Hugo Riemann, "Degeneration und Regeneration in der Musik," in *Max Hesses Deutscher Musikerkalender für das Jahr 1908* (Leipzig, 1908), reprinted in Shigihara, ed., *"Die Konfusion in der Musik,"* 249.

festations of the neoclassical impulse. Their views anticipate by well over a decade the ways in which Hindemith, Stravinsky, and others would advocate the "purity," the "sanity" of Bach as an antidote to much that was deemed unhealthy in the culture of Europe after World War I.[34] These attitudes bring us face to face with what Richard Taruskin has called the "darker side" of modernism, which includes an all-too-close dalliance with anti-Semitism, misogyny, and fascism.[35] The descriptions of physical and mental weakness or sickness in table 1 are indeed typical of the coded anti-Semitic discourse around 1900.[36]

These are important issues for historians of Bach reception to confront, but they take us beyond the immediate scope of this essay. My point has been to suggest that although Brahms's reception of Bach was hardly free of cultural and political ideology, the Bach reception of succeeding generations differed in ways that reflect—and, more significantly, may even have contributed to—the rise of musical modernism.

34. Something of this phenomenon is explored by Richard Taruskin in "Back to Whom? Neoclassicism as Ideology," *Nineteenth-Century Music* 16 (1993): 286–302. Taruskin argues that "there was a Bach of the Left and a Bach of the Right" (297), that is, a Bach claimed by such figures as Hindemith as a society-conscious *Gebrauchsmusiker* and one claimed by elitists like Stravinsky as a more refined, elevated artist.

35. Richard Taruskin, "The Darker Side of Modern Music," *The New Republic*, 5 September 1988, 28–34; and Taruskin, "Back to Whom?" 294.

36. The writings of Sander Gilman explore the language and culture of fin-de-siècle anti-Semitism with particular force. See his *Difference and Pathology* (Ithaca: Cornell University Press, 1985); *The Jew's Body* (New York: Routledge, 1991); and *Freud, Race, and Gender* (Princeton: Princeton University Press, 1993). For a cogent synthesis of Gilman's work and other relevant literature, see K. M. Knittel, " 'Ein hypermoderner Dirigent': Mahler and Anti-Semitism in *Fin-de-siècle* Vienna," *Nineteenth-Century Music* 18 (1995): 257–76 (esp. 259–67).

# Hindemith, Bach, and the Melancholy of Obligation

### Stephen Hinton

I n the middle of preparing for the Hindemith Centenary Celebrations in 1995, I received a letter from a member of a well-known American symphony orchestra who, in the course of announcing his orchestra's own minifestival, boldly apostrophized Hindemith as the "Bach of the Twentieth Century." I had to look no further. Here was vindication, if ever it was needed, for this paper's topic. Not only had Hindemith been affected or influenced by Bach (with or without anxiety), he had actually *become* Bach! Yet the boldness of the phrase also begged a huge question. What does it mean to be Bach in the twentieth century? How had Hindemith achieved this feat of reincarnation?

As Hans Heinrich Eggebrecht pointed out in his paper "Bach—wer ist das?" no composer has been more prone to the image, or *Bild*, syndrome than Bach.[1] Compared to *Bilder* of other composers, the Bach-*Bilder* are legion. What, in other words, was my correspondent's image of Bach, and how did it manage, with the aid of time-traveling, to merge with his image of Hindemith? In my reply, I eagerly included a query about the provenance of the phrase, but to no avail. It was up to me to get to the bottom of this remarkable piece of reception history. I make no apologies to my correspondent for misconstruing his meaning. He had his opportunity for exegesis, and squandered it.

I would like to thank Giselher Schubert, director of the Paul Hindemith Institute (Frankfurt/Main), for generously sharing his expert knowledge of Hindemith's oeuvre and supplying materials from the Institute archive for the preparation of this essay.

1. Hans Heinrich Eggebrecht, "Bach—wer ist das?" *Archiv für Musikwissenschaft* 42 (1985): 216–28.

Hindemith had his opportunities too, of course. Yet he hardly squandered them. In fact, they could seem, even on the briefest inspection, to have been so numerous that their actual enumeration begins to look like the outline for a large book rather than a paper. How would such a book-length study be organized? Somewhere one would be obliged to find room for what would count, chronologically, as the first substantial exhibit in a rich documentation of Hindemith's Bach reception, namely, the posthumously published orchestral piece *Ragtime wohltemperiert*, also available in an arrangement for piano duet. In a note appended to the score, Hindemith wastes no time in introducing the reincarnation idea, albeit in the hypothetical: "Do you suppose Bach is turning in his grave? He wouldn't think of it! If Bach were alive today, perhaps he would have invented the shimmy or at least introduced it into decent music. Perhaps he would have also drawn on a theme from the Well-Tempered Clavier by the kind of composer who would have represented Bach for him."

In other words, if Bach were alive when Hindemith wrote those words (in 1921), he would be Hindemith. Granted, Hindemith didn't invent the shimmy either, but he did introduce popular dance music into the sphere of so-called decent music, most famously in the final movement of his *Kammermusik* no. 1, into which he inserts a fox-trot by Wilm Wilm.[2] And here in the *Ragtime* —both aesthetically and stylistically a kind of companion piece to the first *Kammermusik*, also written in 1921—he stages a similar confrontation between modish dance music and "decent" music. As far as the musical material is concerned, the confrontation amounts to a kind of synthesis: Hindemith takes the theme of the C-minor fugue from Book 1 of the Well-Tempered Clavier and, by simply dotting the first note of the first three eighth-note pairs, deftly transforms the theme into a ragtime—or what he thought was a rag (see ex.1).[3] But the overall effect can hardly be called one of synthesis. The origin of the theme and its new, rather raucous, context are too incongruous for that. It is rather as

2. See Michael Kube, "Paul Hindemith's Jazz-Rezeption: Stationen einer Episode," *Musiktheorie* 10 (1995): 61–71.

3. The ragged rhythms, repeated strains, and syncopations characteristic of ragtime are absent here. The dotted-note figure (which Hindemith also employs in the first *Kammermusik*) became typical in the second decade of the twentieth century because of its association with the fox-trot. Musically, Hindemith is invoking "white" social dance music rather than jig piano. For a historical survey of the term "ragtime," especially in a German context, see Jürgen Hunkemöller, "Was ist Ragtime?" *Archiv für Musikwissenschaft* 42 (1985): 69–86.

EX.1. Paul Hindemith, *Ragtime* (wohltemperiert) for piano, four hands (1921), Schott ED 7325, Mainz: B Schotts Söhne, 1986, mm.24–27

EX.2. Hindemith, *Ragtime*, mm.123–26

though Hindemith were painting a moustache on an old master, even if the obverse is actually the case: apart from grafting the fugue theme onto his orchestral ragtime, Hindemith also interpolates the B–A–C–H motto just before the end, albeit not at proper pitch, at least initially; it begins as G–F♯–A–G♯ (or G–Fis–A–Gis), whatever that might signify beyond Bach, only to become B–A–C–H a few measures later (see ex.2). The gesture, however construed, seems intentionally impertinent. Had the *Ragtime* been given its first performance when it was written, instead of in 1987, some of the more conservative critics might well have reacted with the kind of blimpish outrage with which they greeted the first *Kammermusik* and suggested that Bach should indeed be turning in his grave.[4] Hindemith was at least right to broach the question, however ironically.

Those familiar with the fox-trot finale of the first *Kammermusik* will appreciate the family resemblance: especially the high-energy *Fortspinnung* of Hindemith's triplets juxtaposed with the dotted rhythms of the theme, which is not so much integrated into the texture as pasted in as one of several elements in a montage, suggesting a superficial connection to Stravinsky (see

4. The first performance took place in Berlin on 21 March 1987 as part of the "Berliner Hindemith-Tage." The papers given at the colloquium during the festival, which was devoted to the composer's early works, and a number of concert reviews are collected in *Hindemith-Jahrbuch* 16 (1987).

135

ex.3). Hindemith's Bach reception, as documented here, goes hand in hand with his jazz reception. As such, it belongs in the broader context of a whole group of early works in which he seems to be testing the limits of "decent music" and its putative opposites. A year before composing *Ragtime*, he wrote to his publisher with the following question: "Can you use foxtrots, bostons, rags and other kitsch? I always write such stuff when no more decent music occurs to me. They turn out very well, and I'd imagine you can do better business with such a piece than with my best chamber music. (Good kitsch is something quite rare.)"[5] Kitsch, then, is not bad music, if it is done well, but for Hindemith it is not "decent music" either. If in *Ragtime* Bach epitomizes the height of decency, which I believe he (or it) does, then the piece's principal point is one of provocation, represented by the rude union of decent music and kitsch—an enterprise of Dadaist pedigree, analogous to the appearance of the fox-trot and siren in a piece given the "decent" title of "Kammermusik." The well-known *Suite 1922* belongs to this group of works too.

Hindemith's Dadaist tendencies, soon to disappear from his compositions but not from his drawings, would come back to haunt him in the 1930s, as is

5. Letter to Schott-Verlag, dated 22 March 1920; in Paul Hindemith, *Briefe*, ed. Dieter Rexroth (Frankfurt am Main: Fischer, 1982), 92.

well known.[6] Furtwängler, in his sincere but wrongheaded defense of Hindemith against Nazi slander, would try to excuse them as "sins of youth"—a phrase that curiously resurfaces in Hindemith's own assessment of the *Suite* from 1940. Recently arrived in the United States, he wrote to Schott's in London concerning the firm's plan to reissue the piece, which had originally been published with the composer's own George Grosz–like drawing. "I think," he said, "it is not necessary to reprint that awful Suite 1922, [n]either with picture [n]or without. The piece is really not an honorable ornament in the music-history of our time, and it depresses an old man rather seriously [Hindemith was 45!] to see that just the sins of his youth impress the people more than his better creations."[7]

In a sense, then, Hindemith came to disapprove of the "sin" he had knowingly committed against the "decent music" represented by Bach. This makes the role of Bach in his early music somewhat complicated. In *Ragtime wohltemperiert* he invokes with Bach's help a set of cultural values, not ones he embraces unequivocally so much as the whole tradition of German art music whose virtues are being held up to lighthearted scrutiny. In that sense, too, I would qualify, and suggest a refinement to, Hermann Danuser's reading of *Ragtime* as presented in his 1985 *Hindemith-Jahrbuch* article on "Der Klassiker als Janus." Danuser's purpose in that article is to compare Hindemith's early image of Bach with his later one. His findings present changes (*Wandlungen*) in that image, based on the historical dichotomy of fundamentally opposed aesthetic viewpoints. The dichotomy in question is the one elucidated by the musicologist Heinrich Besseler, which became central to music aesthetics in the Weimar Republic, as I have outlined elsewhere.[8] (In that sense, I am partly responsible for Danuser's reading.) Based on his studies of early music and Heideggerian phenomenology, Besseler contrasted music presented in concerts for the purposes of what he calls aesthetic listening with the more primordial approach of active involvement. The former approach, which he

6. Writing about the *Kammermusik* No. 1, Ian Kemp nicely described Hindemith's musical relationship to Dadaism as "trespassing on the preserves of Dada"; in Ian Kemp, *Hindemith* (Oxford: Oxford University Press, 1970), 11.

7. Letter from Hindemith to Schott (London), quoted in Kube, "Paul Hindemith's Jazz-Rezeption," 71.

8. Stephen Hinton, *The Idea of Gebrauchsmusik* (New York: Garland, 1989).

identifies as belonging to a historically relatively late stage, Besseler called *eigenständige Musik* (autonomous music); the latter type he called *Gebrauchs-musik* or *umgangsmäßige Musik* (utility or vernacular music), which he associ-ates with earlier music as well as with contemporary popular music, includ-ing jazz.[9] Later, retaining the conceptual dualism, Besseler changed the terms to *Darbietungsmusik* (literally, presentation music) and *Umgangsmusik*.[10] In-voking Besseler's distinction between these two fundamental types, and using the later terminology, Danuser asserts that "for Hindemith in 1921 Bach is a model for 'Umgangsmusik,' not for 'Darbietungsmusik.'" Seen in this way, Bach becomes a prototype for a general trend in 1920s aesthetics, one that has frequently been encapsulated in the slogan "Back to Bach," and that is synony-mous in Danuser's reading with "Back to 'Umgangsmusik.'" The equation, I would argue, is too neat to reflect the complexities of Bach reception, whether in Hindemith's own case or a fortiori in that of other composers at the time.

In the first place, there are really two Bachs in Hindemith's introductory words to *Ragtime:* the hypothetical reincarnation figure and the composer of the fugue theme whom the reincarnation figure might, if he existed, see as a Bach-like figure. It is the latter figure, the Bach-like figure, who interests us in the composition itself, for he is in fact the real Bach, or at least Hinde-mith's version of him. He stands for the whole sphere of "decent music" and its attendant values. Yet they are hardly the values that Besseler would associate with *Umgangsmusik;* if anything, quite the contrary. It is the world of ragtime, not the original fugue theme, that is *Umgangsmusik*, invoked at a remove from aesthetic immediacy. This is not to say that Bach's music cannot have that sig-nificance as well, but that it does not do so in this piece.

Hindemith's choice of theme—a fugue—also means something quite dif-ferent from what it would mean later in his career. Fugue as a compositional technique might be the height of "decent" art, but it also stands in the early works, somewhat pejoratively, for dry, even soulless academicism. If, as Gisel-her Schubert has suggested, fugues and fugatos in early Hindemith serve a "programmatic purpose," it is a purpose pursued with characteristic humor

---

9. Heinrich Besseler, "Grundfragen des musikalischen Hörens," *Jahrbuch der Musikbibliothek Peters für 1925* (Leipzig: Peters, 1926), 35–52.

10. "Das musikalische Hören der Neuzeit," *Berichte über die Verhandlungen der Sächsischen Akad-emie der Wissenschaften zu Leipzig, Philosophisch-historische Klasse*, vol. 155 (Berlin, 1959).

of the schoolboyish kind, balancing academic facility with nose-thumbing—
something quite at odds with the later demonstrations of prodigious craftsmanship such as in *Ludus tonalis*.[11] The earlier display, balancing academic
facility with nose-thumbing, is perfectly captured in the "Note for the listener
and the reader of the score" that introduces the third of the three dance pieces
from the 1920 one-act opera *Das Nusch-Nuschi*: "The following 'choral fugue'
(with every luxury: augmentations, diminutions, strettos, bass ostinato) owes
its existence merely to an unhappy circumstance: it occurred to the composer.
Its purpose is nothing other than this: to fit stylishly into the scene and to
afford all cognoscenti the opportunity to yap about the creator's monstrous
lack of taste. Hallelujah! The piece, for the main part, has to be danced (or
wabbled) by two monstrously fat naked bellies."[12]

Chronologically, it is a short step from such programmatic nose-thumbing
at the traditions of decent music to the full-blown neobaroque character of
Hindemith's middle-Weimar years, beginning with the *Kammermusik* no.2 of
1924 and continuing through the remaining five of the set, which (excluding
the first) have been dubbed Hindemith's "Brandenburg Concertos."[13] Not that
there are too many obvious parallels to Bach's concertos themselves, although

11. Giselher Schubert, "Paul Hindemith und der Neobarock: Historische und stilistische Notizen," *Hindemith-Jahrbuch* 12 (1983): 20–40.

12. The late Michael Zimmermann drew attention to Hindemith's use of fugato in his early
works, in particular a passage in the first movement of the String Quartet op.10 and another
in the finale of the Viola Sonata op.11/4, remarking how such passages evince a kind of "de-
semanticization" (*Entsemantisierung*) of music. In both cases, Hindemith supplies performance
instructions that support such a reading: in the first case "completely apathetic, without feeling" (*gänzlich apathetisch, empfindungslos*); in the latter "with bizarre crassness" (*mit bizarrer
Plumpheit*). Zimmermann, with critical intention, likened the effect of such "motoric tootling"
to that of meaningless punning. See his article "Harmlosigkeit und Melancholie bei Christian
Morgenstern und Paul Hindemith," *Hindemith-Jahrbuch* 16 (1987): 58–72.

13. In his liner notes for the recording of the *Kammermusiken* conducted by Ricardo Chailly
(London 433 816-2), Malcolm MacDonald has written: "In the *Kammermusik* series, . . .
[Hindemith] defined . . . an influential Neo-classical impulse in contemporary German music,
just as Igor Stravinsky in Paris was issuing the rallying cry of 'Back to Bach!' Indeed, in one
sense, Hindemith's seven *Kammermusik* compositions—the first of them a suite for twelve instruments, the others concertos for a variety of solo instruments, with orchestras of different
sizes and constitutions—are a kind of twentieth-century equivalent of J. S. Bach's *Brandenburg
Concertos*."

the six pieces are all concertos. The first movement of the second, for example, seems closely modeled on the theme of Bach's Bb-major Two-Part Invention, projected through "the acoustic equivalent of a distorting mirror," as Franz Willms aptly put it in 1925.[14] It is rather that the music's overall effect invokes many of the gestures generally associated with Baroque concerto style—the switching between ripieno and concertino; the homogeneity of texture and basic pulse, or *Einheitsablauf*, as Besseler called it; the progression by sequence; the linear counterpoint (the contemporaneous term coined by Ernst Kurth to describe Bach's music); and so forth.

Aesthetically, on the other hand, the step from the spirit of the *Kammermusik* no. 1 to no. 2 is potentially huge. If the earlier work derives its impact from a willful confrontation between the cultural practices of *Umgangs-* and *Darbietungsmusik*, popular dance music and cerebral Bach, then the slightly later music is hardly *Umgangsmusik* in Besseler's strict sense of the term either. If anything, the reverse is the case. Besseler's conceptual dualism defines, in essence, the phenomenological dimension of the music: how do we approach it, what is our relationship to it? In that sense, the music still belongs to the sphere of *Darbietungsmusik*, not *Umgangsmusik*. And yet, although it hardly signals a return to the earlier model, as Hindemith's amateur music assuredly would, the invocation of the alternative approach is nonetheless essential. The aesthetic program is rather one of postromanticism, even postexpressionism, which defines itself as much negatively as it does positively. Seen in this negative way, the "Back-to-Bach" neobaroqueisms of the *Kammermusiken* are, broadly speaking, antisymphonic. The linear *Einheitsablauf* of the concerto style, with its sequentially repeated figurations, represents a form of abstinence: from functional harmony, from complex syntax, from developing variation and motivic refinement—in short, from late-Romantic expressivity and metaphysics. While challenging the traditions of *Darbietungsmusik*, the music is, positively defined, *umgangsmäßig* only in the sense that, like much of Stravinsky's music from this time, it is performative, ostentatiously putting the performer and the act of music-making on display. Yet, for this very reason, the sonic patterns that the performer weaves enjoy a kind of musical autonomy greater than that of the

14. Franz Willms, "Paul Hindemith: Ein Versuch," *Von neuer Musik: Beiträge zur Erkenntnis der neuzeitlichen Tonkunst*, ed. H. Grues et al. (Cologne: F. J. Marcan, 1925), 101.

late-Romantic *Weltanschauungsmusik* that they specifically oppose.[15] In other words, after music has tasted the fruits of autonomy, understood as a historical practice, there can be no literal going-back to Bach or to *Umgangsmusik* in the philosophical or cultural sense of Besseler's term. Any allusion or borrowing is highly artificial: a protest within the aesthetic sphere rather than from without. To sum up: Bach in early Hindemith has a polemical function.

As mentioned, Hindemith pursues the *Umgangsmusik* ideal most rigorously in his compositions for amateur music-making circles. He was not alone here, of course, nor indeed was Bach the sole prototype. But the *Gebrauchsmusik* movement does furnish the context for a Bach reception in the late Weimar Republic that emphasizes what Wilibald Gurlitt, himself a Besseler pupil, would have called cultural *Gebundenheit* (connectedness).[16] Bach's example as cantata composer plays a central role here. Such a reception finds its most succinct expression in Kurt Weill's 1930 response to a questionnaire entitled "Commitment to Bach" (*Bekenntis zu Bach*): "Whenever we say today 'Art must be useful. But it must also uphold its standards,' then Bach provides the best evidence for the validity of this demand. For him these two concepts are inseparable. His work possesses the highest degree of purposefulness [*Zweckmäßigkeit*]. For (and not despite) this reason, it upholds a unique standard."[17] (Weill, incidentally, also cited Bach's recitatives as an example of gestic music.)[18] Compositionally, Brecht's "Lehrstücke," most obviously those writ-

---

15. The term "Weltanschauungsmusik," denoting late-Romantic music with deep philosophical and metaphysical aspirations and claims, was coined by Rudolf Stephan.

16. Wilibald Gurlitt, "Zur gegenwärtigen Orgelerneuerungsbewegung in Deutschland" (1929), in *Musikgeschichte und Gegenwart*, vol. 2, ed. H. H. Eggebrecht (Wiesbaden: Steiner, 1966), 100. Gurlitt made direct parallels between contemporaneous developments and medieval music. His pupil Besseler reported Gurlitt's taking as the premise of his work the idea of the "*Gebundenheit* [literally: religiosity] of medieval existence," from which he derived an intimate connection between art and life. See Heinrich Besseler, "Musik des Mittelalters in der Hamburger Musikhalle," *Zeitschrift für Musikwissenschaft* 7 (1924–25): 43.

17. Kurt Weill, "Bekenntnis zu Bach," in his *Musik und Theater: Gesammelte Schriften*, ed. Stephen Hinton and Jürgen Schebera (Berlin: Henschel, 1990), 75–76; the questionnaire was originally published in *Die Musik* 22 (1929/30), with responses from, among others, Walter Gieseking and Ernst Toch.

18. "Über den gestischen Charakter der Musik," in *Musik und Theater*, 65: "We find gestic

ten in collaboration with Hanns Eisler, but also those with Weill and Hindemith, draw on Bach's cantatas as prototypes of community-building polyphony—a sociological perspective suggested as early as 1916 by the critic Paul
Bekker.[19]

The study of Hindemith and Bach being outlined here has scarcely got
under way. Hindemith is about thirty; there are another thirty-eight years to
go in his multifaceted career as composer, performer, and pedagogue. Compositionally, one could trace many allusions of varying degrees of specificity;
relevant work here has been done by Günther Metz, David Neumeyer, Rudolf
Stephan, and Richard Taruskin.[20] As a string player, Hindemith frequently
performed Bach, though to my knowledge none of the major Hindemith col-
lections possesses a single recording of any such performance. From the pedagogical angle, there are the analyses of Bach that Hindemith prepared for
his theory book *Unterweisung im Tonsatz*—the one eventually included in the
book (Three-Part Invention in F Minor) and the one that was not (Fugue in
D Major from Book 1 of the Well-Tempered Clavier).[21] (See ex. 4.)

---

music everywhere human interaction is musically represented in a naive fashion. Most strikingly: in the recitatives of Bach's Passions, in Mozart's operas, in *Fidelio* ('Nur hurtig fort und
frisch gegraben'), in Offenbach and Bizet."

19. Paul Bekker, *Das Deutsche Musikleben* (Berlin: Schuster & Loeffler, 1916); see also Helga
de la Motte-Haber, "Grenzüberschreitung als Sinngebung in der Musik des 20. Jahrhunderts,"
in *Musik und Religion*, ed. H. de la Motte-Haber (Laaber: Laaber, 1995), 217–49. On the connection between Bach's Passions and the didactic plays of Weill, Eisler, and other composers
during the Weimar Republic, see Stephen Hinton, "*Lehrstück:* An Aesthetics of Performance,"
in *Music and Performance in the Weimar Republic*, ed. Bryan Gilliam (Cambridge: Cambridge
University Press, 1994), 59–73; reprinted in *Hindemith-Jahrbuch* 22 (1993): 68–96.

20. Günter Metz, "Hindemith und die Alte Musik," in *Alte Musik im 20. Jahrhundert: Wandlungen und Formen ihrer Rezeption*, ed. Giselher Schubert (Mainz: Schott, 1995), 93–112; David
Neumeyer, "Hindemith's *hommages à Bach* in Two Early Viola Sonatas," *Hindemith-Jahrbuch* 26
(1987): 153–74; Rudolf Stephan, "Der frühe Hindemith," *Hindemith-Jahrbuch* 26 (1987): 9–17;
Richard Taruskin, "In Search of the 'Good' Hindemith Legacy," *New York Times*, 8 January 1995.

21. For commentary on Hindemith's analysis of the F-minor Invention (BWV 795), see Werner
Breig, "Zur Harmonik von Bachs f-moll Sinfonia," in *Festschrift Erich Doflein zum 70. Geburtstag*, ed. Lars Ulrich Abraham (Mainz: Schott, 1972), 17–26. I am grateful to Giselher Schubert
of the Hindemith-Institut for supplying a copy of Hindemith's unpublished analysis of Bach's
D-major fugue.

EX. 4. J. S. Bach, Fugue in D Major from Book 1 of the Well-Tempered Clavier, unpublished harmonic analysis by Paul Hindemith, ca. 1935, prepared for but not included in the 1937 theory book *Unterweisung im Tonsatz*. Reproduced by permission of the Paul Hindemith Institute (Frankfurt/Main).

Constraints of space require me to skip to 1950, to my other principal document, the speech entitled "Johann Sebastian Bach: Ein verpflichtendes Erbe" (Johann Sebastian Bach and the obligation of heritage), which Hindemith gave in Hamburg on 12 September 1950 as part of the anniversary festivities.[22] The speech came in the middle of the program, rather than acting as a preamble to it, appearing after Bach's Prelude and Fugue in C Major for Organ and Hindemith's own *Apparebit repentina dies* for mixed chorus and winds and before Bach's Magnificat. Hindemith also conducted. Wherever the speech finds mention in our hypothetical large-scale study, whether at the outset or in the chronologically correct position in his career at the beginning of his so-called late period, it would presumably have to be discussed in terms of the radical contrast it presents with the composer's earlier Bach reception. Such, as suggested, is Danuser's approach in his *Hindemith-Jahrbuch* article, in which the relationship to Bach figures as the mirror or mouthpiece of Hindemith's own compositional aesthetic. The job of doing reception history would naturally tend towards such an interpretation—to view the Bach speech principally, if not exclusively, as what Danuser calls Hindemith's "attempt at defining his own position" (*Versuch einer eigenen Standortbestimmung*).[23] How could it not be so? Yet at the opening of his speech, seemingly mindful of such a potential charge, Hindemith addresses the issue head on. This is the paradox that emerges: If he is defining his own position, he is doing so expressly with the intention of cutting through the layers of reception history and, as far as possible, transcending even his own perspective—an intention with which many Bach researchers can presumably sympathize, even if they must ultimately find the goal a chimerical one. Like Eggebrecht thirty-five years later, Hindemith finds himself searching for an answer to the question: "Bach—wer ist das?" *My* question is this: In his search for the "real Bach," as he calls him—"the true figure of the man Bach and his work"—is Hindemith unveiling just another image of Bach among many or something more essential and lasting than that?

Although the distance he adopts from the hypothetical reincarnation of the

22. Paul Hindemith, *Johann Sebastian Bach: Ein verpflichtendes Erbe* (Mainz: Schott, 1950); reprinted in Paul Hindemith, *Aufsätze—Vorträge—Reden* (Zurich: Atlantis, 1994), 253–70; trans. by Stanley Godman as *Johann Sebastian Bach: Heritage and Obligation* (London: Oxford University Press; New Haven: Yale University Press, 1952).

23. Hermann Danuser, "Der Klassiker als Janus," *Hindemith-Jahrbuch* 14 (1985): 14.

*Ragtime* note could scarcely be greater, his opening strategy in his Bach speech is curiously similar. He wonders how Bach might have reacted to his most recent reception, were he still around. As a response Hindemith suggests that Bach would, by now, have ceased being startled: "What further strange things could confront him, his having been turned fifteen years ago as an anti-church composer into a pillar of brown Germany and only recently, with the help of the Chinese minister of culture, into a pioneer for red internationalism? With, in the two hundred years since his death, each generation wanting to see him transformed; pulling, analyzing, explaining and commenting on him hither and thither in his works; incorporating him into every household in books, pictures and plaster busts; in short, with his becoming a monument."[24]

There are various ways Hindemith proposes to dismantle the monument and get back to "the true figure of the man Bach and his works." One is a practical suggestion: that performers make use of Bach's autographs, presented in facsimile alongside the engraved edited version. Other aspects of his approach to performance are similarly informed by a desire to return to origins. Hindemith, like Joshua Rifkin and others, argues for an appreciation of the small-scale forces used to perform Bach's choral works.[25] "We can be certain," he says, "that Bach felt quite comfortable with the vocal and stylistic means at his disposal, and if we aim to present his music as he envisaged it, then we must reconstruct the performance conditions of the time."[26] For Hindemith, this also meant restringing the string instruments, using wind instruments of a size comparable to the ones originally used, and also reconstructing the appropriate tuning. Here, then, is an early voice propagating—dare I say it?—authenticity.

His efforts were not always appreciated unequivocally, even by his admirers. Here is Arthur Mendel, the translator of the *Unterweisung im Tonsatz*, recalling Hindemith's approach:

> Hindemith had particularly strong convictions about the subordination of the role of the performer to that of the composer, and he made it a point to emphasize this in every way he could. [Mendel later describes Hindemith's insistence on using the viola d'amore and the gamba in the St. John Passion, even with

24. Hindemith, "Johann Sebastian Bach: Ein verpflichtendes Erbe," *Aufsätze—Vorträge—Reden*, 253–54.

25. Joshua Rifkin, "Bach's Chorus: A Preliminary Report," *Musical Times* 123 (1982): 747–51.

26. Hindemith, "Johann Sebastian Bach: Ein verpflichtendes Erbe," 258.

players unfamiliar with these instruments.] Sometimes I thought that he exaggerated this, as, for example, when I heard him conduct the B-minor Mass in Düsseldorf in 1956. He had always particularly belittled conductors and conducting, and he seemed bent on this occasion, too, on proving that all you had to do was get the right notes sounded at the right time and everything else would take care of itself—or had been taken care of by the composer. The performance was painfully "straight," and seemed to me to succeed in suppressing almost all that sensitivity to the subtlest inflections which, from long acquaintance, I knew Hindemith had in superlative degree.[27]

One could argue that it is as much Hindemith the performer as Hindemith the composer who favored such subordination. At any rate, the contrast with the approach to the performance of Bach's music by other modern composers such as Mahler, Busoni, and the Second Viennese School could scarcely be more pronounced. All of these last favored some kind of creative intervention. Mahler and Schoenberg both prepared, to greater and lesser degrees, instrumental retouchings, or *Retuschen*.[28] And Busoni, both as arranger and composer, with his essentially Romantic approach, predicated as it was on the notion of an always sonically absent *Urmusik*, intentionally blurs any precise distinction between edition, arrangement, and *Nachdichtung*.[29]

It is in this connection that Adorno's characteristically titled piece "Bach Defended against his Devotees" should be mentioned. In it, from his Second Viennese perspective, Adorno passed scathing judgment on Hindemith's Hamburg speech of a year earlier. By way of an apology for Webern's orchestral arrangements, Adorno ends by summarizing his position vis-à-vis our obligation to Bach's heritage in radical contrast to Hindemith's position: "Perhaps

27. "Recollections of Hindemith," *American Choral Review* 6, no. 3 (1964): 5–7.

28. Cf. the recent Yale dissertation: Julie Hubbert, "Mahler and Schoenberg: Levels of Influence" (Ph.D. diss., Yale University, 1996).

29. Busoni uses the heavily idealistic term *Urmusik* (with which he associates most closely the music of Beethoven and Bach) in his *Entwurf einer neuen Ästhetik der Tonkunst* (1907; 2/1916). Elsewhere, of course, he is constantly obsessed with the essence of music, something unattainable by mere composition or performance. *Urmusik*—analogous to, but because of its incorporeality quite different from, Heinrich Schenker's *Urlinie*—is, as it were, the music behind actual music. In that sense, there is only a gradual, not an absolute, difference between composition and interpretation; each amounts to an always necessarily imperfect realization of *Urmusik*, itself as much as unattainable goal as an unfathomable origin.

Bach as transmitted has actually become uninterpretable. In which case his heritage falls to the act of composing, which remains faithful to him by being unfaithful, and identifies that heritage's content by recreating it for itself." [30] But it is Hindemith's view of Bach's late style in particular that Adorno lambasts, describing it as "a grotesque misunderstanding" (*grotesk verkannt*).[31] This is not the place to take issue with Adorno's own anachronisms, instructive though such an inquiry might be. Hindemith's will have to suffice. For Bach scholars, Hindemith's view of Bach could seem not so much anachronistic in the precise sense of that term (although it is that too) as almost prophetic, anticipating the "new picture" of Bach outlined by Friedrich Blume over a decade later.[32] When he gave the speech (in 1950), Hindemith would not have had the benefit of the new chronology of Bach's works that emerged during the next decade, establishing earlier dates for some of the compositions previously included among the late works. It is the results of this research, Blume argued, that led him to talk of the final decade in terms of Bach's "collecting and preserving and also of transmitting the tradition which he had received, of [continuing] a tradition of consummate contrapuntal skill." All of this Blume described in terms of an "esoteric activity." [33]

Hindemith goes further, with less evidence, than Blume. For his part, perhaps he needed no more than the writings of Birnbaum and Scheibe to reach his conclusions. But the parallel between Blume's and Hindemith's interpretations does raise a prickly question where biographical interpretation enters the picture. How much did the findings of the new research produce a new image of Bach, and how much, conversely, did the image of Bach produce the findings?

There can be no simple answer here; the process is necessarily two-sided. It is an issue that admits of no easy resolution, involving as it does matters to do with influence and reception. How much was Hindemith influenced by Bach? Or conversely: How much, in his reception, did he construct his picture of Bach, so to speak, in his own image? In other words, was Blume's esoteric picture of Bach one that suited postwar German Bach reception in the

---

30. Theodor W. Adorno, "Bach gegen seine Liebhaber verteidigt," *Prismen*; reprinted in his *Gesammelte Schriften*, vol.10/1 (Frankfurt am Main: Suhrkamp, 1977), 138–51.

31. Ibid., 144.

32. Friedrich Blume, "Outlines of a New Picture of Bach," *Music and Letters* 44 (1963): 214–27.

33. Ibid., 226.

same way that it suited Hindemith—and suited him to the extent that, for all his professed desire to get to the "real" Bach (or perhaps even because, like Blume, he is presenting a biographical interpretation), he ends up giving us a mirror image of Hindemith? The matter of wishful construction seems especially blatant and rich at the point in the 1950 speech that provides my title, that is, where Hindemith introduces the concept of melancholy. He does so with the help of Nietzsche, transforming the maliciously negative expression Nietzsche used to describe Brahms into a positive one to describe late Bach. Where Nietzsche, in the second addendum to *Der Fall Wagner*, had described Brahms's melancholy as a melancholy of inability, incapacity, or even poverty (*Melancholie des Unvermögens*), Hindemith adapts the phrase to describe Bach's last decade in terms of a "melancholy of ability."[34] How much Hindemith was playing on Nietzsche's lengthy explanation of the phrase, which amounts to a negative feminization of Brahms (he calls him "a musician of the unsatisfied women type"), and how much he intended a slight against a composer about whom he had little good to say, remains unclear.[35] But insofar as his explanation of Bach's melancholy readily applies in its specifics to his own situation, Hindemith is implicitly casting himself not only as an antipode to Brahms but also as the satisfied and capable male.

What does he mean by "melancholy of ability" in Bach's case, a concept he describes as the "answer to all mysteries?" It has to be seen in the context of the idea introduced at the beginning of the speech, where Bach, he says, "creates a world of the work of art completely independent of [his petit-bourgeois

34. Friedrich Nietzsche, *Der Fall Wagner*, in his *Sämtliche Werke*, vol. 6 (Munich: Deutscher Taschenbuch Verlag, 1980), 9–53, at p. 47: "Er [Brahms] hat die Melancholie des Unvermögens; er schafft nicht aus der Fülle, er durstet nach der Fülle"; the Hindemith speech is quoted here from Hindemith, *Aufsätze—Vorträge—Reden*, 267.

35. In 1940 Hindemith wrote to his wife from Buffalo, New York, about two concerts that included music by Brahms. The first was an amateur performance of the *Requiem*: "Since I hadn't heard the piece for a long time, and always forget it, because I don't like it, I listened to it as if it were a new discovery. But not a pleasant one. It's a dismal piece; seeing [Brahms] grumbling on about death and the life to come robs one of any incentive to die. Give me old Giuseppe [Verdi] any day." Of Brahms's Fourth Symphony, included in a concert of the Cleveland Orchestra under Rodzinsky, Hindemith wrote: "with such matter-of-fact treatment the work shows its weaknesses more than ever." Quoted from Paul Hindemith, *"Das private Logbuch": Briefe an seine Frau*, ed. Friederike Becker and Giselher Schubert (Mainz: Schott, 1995), 440–41.

environment]." [36] The dropping off in Bach's productivity, Hindemith argues, is the result of having achieved perfection. The idea of perfection is hardly new, of course. It is a quality already acknowledged by Birnbaum. In his discussion of Birnbaum in the final chapter of his Bach essays, Christoph Wolff aptly describes psychological questions concerning artistic impulse and creativity as belonging to a "nebulous sphere," especially in the case of Bach, given the paucity of relevant documentation. [37] Hindemith's interpretation of Bach's perfection necessarily enters this sphere, particularly where he describes Bach's late period in terms of "the melancholy, the sadness, of having lost all previous imperfections and with them the possibility of further progress." [38] Thus Bach and his music become for Hindemith a symbol of "all that is noble" (*für alles Edle*). It is not hard to draw parallels with how Hindemith felt about his own situation—how he, in contrast to his youthful self, had created works of art "completely independent of his environment." In fact, the very language of the ending of the Bach speech is almost identical to that of his foreword, written two years earlier, to the revised edition of *Das Marienleben*. The vision that informed the revision was "an ideal of noble music, as perfect as possible." Whereas for Bach the melancholy is described primarily in personal psychological terms, for Hindemith the kind of consolation he seeks relates to the general historical situation. "Since Beethoven's death," he writes in the foreword, "we have experienced an uninterrupted ars nova"—an ars nova which cast Hindemith in the 1950s in the role of archconservative. In other words, the melancholy of late Hindemith has what Reinhold Brinkmann has called, fittingly enough in relation to Brahms, a historical "signature" [39]—a signature

36. Hindemith, *Aufsätze—Vorträge—Reden*, 256.

37. Christoph Wolff, "'The Extraordinary Perfections of the Hon. Court Composer': An Inquiry into the Individuality of Bach's Music," in his *Bach: Essays on His Life and Music* (Cambridge, Mass.: Harvard University Press, 1991), 391.

38. Hindemith, *Aufsätze—Vorträge—Reden*, 268-69.

39. Reinhold Brinkmann, *Johannes Brahms: Die Zweite Symphonie* (Munich: Edition Text und Kritik, 1990), 77. See also another article by Brinkmann that deals with late Hindemith from a related perspective: "Über Paul Hindemiths Rede 'Sterbende Gewässer,'" *Hindemith-Jahrbuch* 13 (1984): 71–90. Brinkmann notes an apparent discrepancy between Hindemith's fervent attack on New Music vented in that 1963 speech and his active interest at the time, as conductor and music theorist, in the music of Webern and Berg. Hindemith's polemics, he suggests, could be read as a kind of self-protection. For all the self-assurance of Hindemith's public image,

of anxiety about the place of his own works as, to use Hindemith's own phrase, "ornaments in the music-history of our time."[40] So perhaps the use of Nietzsche's malicious phrase is more complex than it might at first seem. Historically, the not-so-obvious parallel with Brahms is more appropriate than the all-too-obvious one with Bach.

In conclusion, I return to the phrase that got me started: "The Bach of the Twentieth Century." This brief investigation has presented material that accounts for the phrase but that also helps us qualify it. Yet for all the obvious differences between early and late Hindemith, his attitude toward Bach remains remarkably consistent. In *Ragtime wohltemperiert* of 1921, Bach symbolizes the sphere of "decent music," however equivocal Hindemith may have felt about it. In the 1950 Bach speech, "decent music" becomes "noble" and "perfect" music, toward which the composer now openly aspires. Admittedly from quite different standpoints—the one openly provocative, the other conservatively self-defensive—the two documents reveal another consistency in Hindemith's Bach reception as well. This great symbol of European music, as Hindemith saw Bach, is pressed into service as part of a more or less overt cultural polemic. The act of historicization is itself historically specific.

Brinkmann detects an element of artistic isolation and a related capacity for melancholy in the composer's last years.

40. Kube, "Paul Hindemith's Jazz-Rezeption," 71.

# CONTRIBUTORS

THOMAS CHRISTENSEN is an associate professor of music theory at the University of Iowa. He is the author of *Rameau and Musical Thought in the Enlightenment* and editor of the *Cambridge History of Western Music Theory* and *Aesthetics and the Art of Musical Composition in the German Enlightenment: Selected Writings of Johann Georg Sulzer and Heinrich Christoph Koch*.

LUDWIG FINSCHER is professor emeritus of musicology at the University of Heidelberg. He is the author of *Loyset Compere, c. 1450–1518: Life and Works* and *Studien zur Geschichte des Streichquartetts*; he is editor or coeditor of more than twenty books; he is also the general editor of *Musik in Geschichte und Gegenwart*. He has served as president of the Gesellschaft für Musikforschung and of the International Musicological Society.

WALTER FRISCH is a professor of music at Columbia University. He is the author of *Brahms and the Principle of Developing Variation*, *The Early Works of Arnold Schoenberg, 1893–1908*—both of which received an ASCAP-Deems Taylor Award—and *Brahms: The Four Symphonies*; he is editor of *Brahms and His World* and *Schubert: Critical and Analytical Studies*. He has served as editor of the journal *Nineteenth-Century Music* and as president of the American Brahms Society.

STEPHEN HINTON is an associate professor and chair of the Department of Music at Stanford University; he has also taught at Yale University and the Technische Universität Berlin. He is the author of *The Idea of Gebrauchsmusik*, *Kurt Weill: The Threepenny Opera*, and the entries on Weill for the *New Grove Dictionary of Opera*; he is coeditor (with Jürgen Schebera) of *Kurt Weill: Gesammelte Schriften*, and editor of the symphony *Mathis der Maler* for the collected edition of the works of Paul Hindemith. He is a member of the editorial board of the *Kurt Weill Edition* and the *Journal of Music Theory*, and reviews editor for *Beethoven Forum*.

WILLIAM KINDERMAN is a professor of music at the University of Victoria and has also taught extensively at the Hochschule der Künste Berlin. He has published many studies on the music of Mozart, Schubert, Chopin, and Wagner and is the author of *Beethoven* and *Beethoven's Diabelli Variations*; he is editor of

*Beethoven's Compositional Process* and coeditor (with Harald Krebs) of *The Second Practice of Nineteenth-Century Tonality*. He is also a pianist whose recording of Beethoven's "Diabelli" Variations has met with widespread critical acclaim.

MICHAEL MARISSEN is an associate professor of music at Swarthmore College. He is the author of *Lutheranism, Anti-Judaism, and Bach's St. John Passion* and *The Social and Religious Designs of J. S. Bach's Brandenburg Concertos* and coauthor (with Daniel R. Melamed) of *An Introduction to Bach Studies*. He is currently vice-president of the American Bach Society.

ROBERT L. MARSHALL, the Louis, Frances and Jeffrey Sachar Professor of Music at Brandeis University, is the author of *The Compositional Process of J. S. Bach* and *The Music of Johann Sebastian Bach: The Sources, the Style, the Significance*; he is editor of *Eighteenth-Century Keyboard Music* and *Mozart Speaks: Views on Music, Musicians, and the World*. A contributor to the *Neue Bach-Ausgabe*, he has also served as chair of the American Bach Society.

# GENERAL INDEX

# General Index

# INDEX OF BACH'S

# COMPOSITIONS

# Index of Bach's Compositions